ITF+ CompTIA IT Fundamentals

A Step by Step Study Guide to Practice Test Questions With Answers and Master the Exam

Table of Contents

Introduction

Welcome to the world of IT fundamentals, where technology meets proficiency, and knowledge paves the way for success. This book has been meticulously crafted to guide you through the essential concepts and principles of information technology, specifically tailored for the CompTIA IT Fundamentals (ITF+) exam.

In today's rapidly evolving digital landscape, a foundational understanding of IT is more crucial than ever. Whether you're a budding IT professional, a career switcher looking to enter the tech industry, or simply someone eager to enhance your digital literacy, this book serves as your comprehensive companion to mastering the core principles that underpin modern computing.

The CompTIA IT Fundamentals (ITF+) certification is an industry-recognized credential that validates your foundational knowledge of IT concepts and skills. It's a stepping stone for those starting their journey in the vast field of information technology. This book is designed to help you not only grasp the necessary knowledge but also to reinforce your understanding through hands-on practice questions and detailed answers.

Key Features:

- Comprehensive Coverage: Delve into the essential topics covered by the CompTIA ITF+ exam, ensuring that you are well-equipped with the foundational knowledge required in the ever-expanding IT domain.

- Practical Approach: Learn by doing with a plethora of practice questions that simulate the exam environment. Each question is accompanied by detailed explanations, allowing you to reinforce your understanding and identify areas for improvement.

- Real-world Relevance: Connect theoretical concepts to real-world scenarios, enabling you to apply your knowledge in practical situations. The ITF+ certification is not just about passing an exam but acquiring skills that are relevant to the dynamic IT landscape.

- Exam Readiness: Familiarize yourself with the structure and format of the CompTIA ITF+ exam through strategically organized practice questions. Boost your confidence and ensure that you are well-prepared to tackle the certification assessment.

- Accessible Language: Navigate complex IT concepts with ease as the book is written in a clear and accessible language. Whether you're a seasoned professional or a newcomer to the IT world, this book caters to a broad audience.

As you embark on this learning journey, remember that mastering the fundamentals is the cornerstone of success in any field. The skills and knowledge you gain from this book will not only prepare you for the CompTIA IT Fundamentals exam but will also serve as a solid foundation for your future endeavors in the dynamic and exciting realm of information technology. Let the exploration begin!

Chapter 1: IT Concepts and Terminology

1.1 Compare and Contrast Notational Systems

In the realm of information technology, notational systems play a pivotal role in representing and manipulating data. Three prominent notational systems — binary, hexadecimal, and decimal — serve as the foundation for encoding and decoding information within computing systems. Understanding their differences is crucial for IT professionals.

Binary is the fundamental language of computers, utilizing only two digits, 0 and 1, to represent all data. It's the language of machine code, providing a direct correspondence to the physical on/off states of electronic components. Hexadecimal, on the other hand, is a base-16 system that simplifies the representation of binary data by using a combination of numbers (0-9) and letters (A-F). This makes it more human-readable, particularly when dealing with complex binary information.

Decimal, the base-10 system, is the familiar numerical system we use daily. Unlike binary and hexadecimal, it employs ten digits (0-9). While decimal is intuitive for human comprehension, it's less efficient for computers since they primarily operate in binary. Understanding how these notational systems interrelate is fundamental for effective communication between human users and computing machines.

Data representation is the overarching concept that ties these notational systems together. It involves encoding information in a format that can be easily processed and understood by computers. A deep comprehension of these systems empowers IT professionals to navigate the intricacies of data representation, laying the groundwork for efficient data handling in various computing scenarios.

1.2 Compare and Contrast Fundamental Data Types and Their Characteristics

Within the landscape of programming and data processing, fundamental data types are the building blocks for constructing meaningful information. Four primary data types include Char (character), Strings, Numbers, and Boolean.

Char represents individual characters, such as letters or symbols. It's the basic unit for encoding textual information. Strings are sequences of characters and are employed to handle text data more extensively, allowing for the manipulation of words, sentences, or entire documents. Understanding the nuances of Char and Strings is crucial for developing applications that involve text processing.

Numbers encompass various numeric data types, such as integers and floating-point numbers. These types are essential for performing mathematical operations and representing quantities in programming. A solid grasp of numeric data types is fundamental for accurate and efficient computation in software development.

Boolean is a binary data type that can only take on two values: true or false. Boolean data types are pivotal for logical operations and decision-making in programming. They form the basis for conditional statements, loops, and other control structures, influencing the flow of a program's execution.

Understanding the characteristics of these fundamental data types is paramount for effective programming and data manipulation. It lays the groundwork for writing code that not only executes correctly but also accurately represents and processes information in diverse computing contexts.

1.3 Illustrate the Basics of Computing and Processing

Computing and processing are the core functions that define the essence of information technology. This section explores the fundamental concepts of input, processing, output, and storage within the context of computing systems.

Input refers to the data that a computer receives from external sources. It can be in the form of user inputs, sensor readings, or any other data that the system needs to process. Accurate input is crucial for the reliability and effectiveness of computing processes.

Processing involves the manipulation and transformation of input data to produce meaningful output. This step is the heart of computing, where algorithms and instructions are executed to perform specific tasks. Central processing units (CPUs) play a central role in this phase, carrying out arithmetic, logic, and control operations.

Output is the result produced by the processing of input data. It can take various forms, such as displaying information on a screen, generating a printed document, or producing audible signals. The quality of output is directly influenced by the accuracy and efficiency of the processing stage.

Storage is the component that allows computers to retain and recall data. It involves both short-term memory (RAM) and long-term storage (hard drives, SSDs). Effective storage management is critical for preserving data between processing sessions and ensuring the continuity of computing tasks.

By comprehending the intricacies of input, processing, output, and storage, individuals gain a holistic understanding of the computing process. This knowledge is foundational for anyone navigating the complexities of information technology, from software developers crafting efficient algorithms to end-users interacting with computing devices in their daily lives.

1.4 Explain the Value of Data and Information

In the contemporary digital landscape, data and information have become invaluable assets driving innovation, decision-making, and competitive advantage. Recognizing data and information as assets emphasizes their strategic importance to individuals, organizations, and society as a whole. Data, in its raw form, serves as the foundation upon which information is built. The transformation of data into meaningful information enhances its usability and relevance, making it a valuable resource.

Understanding data and information as assets highlights the critical need for investing in security measures. As technology advances, the volume and sensitivity of data increase, making it a prime target for cyber threats. Investment in robust security infrastructure and practices is essential to safeguard data integrity, confidentiality, and availability. By doing so, individuals and organizations can mitigate the risks associated with unauthorized access, data breaches, and other cybersecurity challenges.

The relationship between data and information is symbiotic. Data serves as the raw material, while information represents the processed and contextualized form of that data. The effective utilization of data to create meaningful information is key to extracting insights, making informed decisions, and driving innovation. Intellectual property, including patents, trademarks, and copyrights, underscores the value of information and data-driven innovations, providing legal protection and fostering an environment conducive to creativity and invention.

In the realm of business, digital products are often the result of leveraging data and information effectively. Understanding the nuances of data-driven business decisions empowers organizations to optimize operations, enhance customer experiences, and gain a competitive edge. Recognizing the intrinsic value of data and information is paramount in navigating the digital landscape and harnessing its potential for positive outcomes.

1.5 Compare and Contrast Common Units of Measure

The effective communication and understanding of computing resources involve common units of measure, including storage units, throughput units, and processing speed. These units play a crucial role in quantifying and comparing various aspects of computing performance.

Storage units, such as bytes, kilobytes, megabytes, gigabytes, and terabytes, measure the capacity of data storage. Throughput units, on the other hand, gauge the rate at which data is transferred or processed. This includes units like bits per second (bps), kilobits per second (kbps), megabits per second (mbps), and gigabits per second (gbps). These units are essential for understanding the efficiency and speed of data transfer in networks.

Processing speed, often measured in hertz (Hz) or gigahertz (GHz), quantifies the speed at which a computer's central processing unit (CPU) performs operations. It reflects the processing capacity and determines how quickly a computer can execute instructions.

Comparing and contrasting these units is vital for selecting appropriate hardware configurations, optimizing network performance, and understanding the capabilities of computing devices. Whether assessing the storage capacity of a hard drive, the speed of data transfer in a network, or the processing power of a CPU, a solid grasp of these units is essential for making informed decisions in the realm of information technology.

1.6 Explain the Troubleshooting Methodology

Troubleshooting is a systematic approach to identifying, diagnosing, and resolving issues that arise within computing systems. This methodology ensures that problems are addressed efficiently, minimizing downtime and optimizing system functionality.

Research Knowledge Base/Internet: The troubleshooting process often begins with consulting available resources, such as knowledge bases and the internet. This step involves gathering information about similar issues and potential solutions, leveraging the collective knowledge of the community and industry experts.

Establish a Theory of Probable Cause: Based on the information gathered, a hypothesis or theory of probable cause is formulated. This involves identifying the most likely reasons behind the issue. It guides subsequent steps in the troubleshooting process.

Test the Theory to Determine the Cause: The formulated theory is put to the test through a series of diagnostic steps. This may involve conducting experiments, running diagnostic tools, or examining system logs to validate or invalidate the initial hypothesis.

Establish a Plan of Action to Resolve the Problem and Identify Potential Effects: Once the cause is identified, a plan of action is developed to address the issue. This plan includes not only resolving the problem but also assessing potential side effects and ensuring minimal impact on overall system functionality.

Implement the Solution or Escalate as Necessary: The proposed solution is implemented, and the system is monitored for changes. If the initial solution does not resolve the issue, or if new complications arise, escalation to higher-level support or additional expertise may be necessary.

Verify Full System Functionality and, if Applicable, Implement Preventive Measures: After implementing the solution, the entire system functionality is verified to ensure that the problem is resolved. Additionally, preventive measures may be implemented to mitigate the likelihood of similar issues occurring in the future.

Document Findings/Lessons Learned, Actions, and Outcomes: Finally, a thorough documentation of the troubleshooting process is essential. This includes detailing the identified problem, the steps taken to resolve it, and any lessons learned during the process. This documentation serves as a valuable resource for future reference and contributes to the collective knowledge base.

In essence, the troubleshooting methodology is a dynamic and iterative process that demands a combination of technical expertise, critical thinking, and effective communication skills. Following these systematic steps enhances the efficiency and effectiveness of resolving issues within computing systems.

Practice Question and Answers on IT Concepts and Terminology

1. Which notational system uses base-16 and includes both numbers and letters (A-F)?

a) Binary

b) Decimal

c) Hexadecimal

d) Octal

Answer: c) Hexadecimal

Explanation: Hexadecimal is a base-16 system that uses the digits 0-9 and the letters A-F to represent values. It is commonly used in computing to represent binary-coded values more conveniently.

2. What is the primary function of the binary notational system in computing?

a) Human-readable representation

b) Efficient data storage

c) Machine code representation

d) Decimal calculations

Answer: c) Machine code representation

Explanation: Binary is the fundamental language of computers, representing machine code in the form of 0s and 1s, corresponding to the on/off states of electronic components.

3. Which fundamental data type is used to represent individual characters?

a) Strings

b) Numbers

c) Char

d) Boolean

Answer: c) Char

Explanation: The Char data type is used to represent individual characters, such as letters or symbols.

4. What is the primary purpose of Boolean data type in programming?

a) Text representation

b) Mathematical calculations

c) Logical operations and decision-making

d) Storage optimization

Answer: c) Logical operations and decision-making

Explanation: Boolean data types are used for logical operations and decision-making in programming, where values are either true or false.

5. How is data transformed into meaningful information?

a) Through data encryption

b) Through data analysis and processing

c) Through data compression

d) Through data storage

Answer: b) Through data analysis and processing

Explanation: Data is transformed into meaningful information through analysis and processing, extracting insights and context.

6. Why is investing in security crucial for data and information?

a) To increase data storage capacity

b) To enhance data processing speed

c) To safeguard data integrity, confidentiality, and availability

d) To optimize data retrieval efficiency

Answer: c) To safeguard data integrity, confidentiality, and availability

Explanation: Investing in security is crucial to protect data from unauthorized access, breaches, and other cybersecurity threats.

7. What legal concept provides protection for intellectual property related to information and data-driven innovations?

a) Data protection

b) Digital rights management

c) Intellectual property

d) Cybersecurity laws

Answer: c) Intellectual property

Explanation: Intellectual property laws, such as patents, trademarks, and copyrights, provide legal protection for innovations and creations in the digital realm.

8. What are digital products often a result of in the business context?

a) Random processes

b) Trial and error

c) Leveraging data and information effectively

d) Market trends

Answer: c) Leveraging data and information effectively

Explanation: Digital products are often developed by leveraging data and information effectively to meet market demands.

9. What is the purpose of common units of measure in computing?

a) To confuse users

b) To quantify and compare computing resources

c) To limit computational capabilities

d) To simplify data representation

Answer: b) To quantify and compare computing resources

Explanation: Common units of measure, such as storage units, throughput units, and processing speed, quantify and facilitate the comparison of computing resources.

10. What unit of measure is used to quantify the rate of data transfer or processing speed in a network?

a) Bytes

b) Bits per second (bps)

c) Hertz (Hz)

d) Kilobytes

Answer: b) Bits per second (bps)

Explanation: Throughput units, such as bits per second, measure the rate of data transfer or processing speed in a network.

11. In troubleshooting, what is the initial step when encountering a problem?

a) Implement the solution

b) Test the theory of probable cause

c) Document findings

d) Research the knowledge base/Internet

Answer: d) Research the knowledge base/Internet

Explanation: The initial step in troubleshooting is to gather information and research potential solutions from available resources.

12. What is the purpose of establishing a theory of probable cause in troubleshooting?

a) To implement a solution immediately

b) To identify potential side effects

c) To test the theory's accuracy

d) To escalate the issue

Answer: c) To test the theory's accuracy

Explanation: Establishing a theory of probable cause in troubleshooting is followed by testing to determine its accuracy in identifying the root cause of the problem.

13. What is the primary focus of testing the theory during troubleshooting?

a) To identify potential side effects

b) To escalate the issue

c) To implement preventive measures

d) To determine the cause of the problem

Answer: d) To determine the cause of the problem

Explanation: Testing the theory in troubleshooting is focused on identifying the cause of the problem.

14. Why is it important to establish a plan of action in troubleshooting?

a) To escalate the issue

b) To document findings

c) To identify potential side effects

d) To resolve the problem and minimize impact

Answer: d) To resolve the problem and minimize impact

Explanation: Establishing a plan of action in troubleshooting is essential to efficiently resolve the problem and minimize its impact on overall system functionality.

15. What is the final step in the troubleshooting methodology?

a) Document findings/lessons learned, actions, and outcomes

b) Verify full system functionality

c) Establish a theory of probable cause

d) Research the knowledge base/Internet

Answer: a) Document findings/lessons learned, actions, and outcomes

Explanation: The final step in troubleshooting is documenting the entire process, including findings, actions taken, and lessons learned for future reference.

16. How does the troubleshooting methodology contribute to system reliability?

a) By implementing solutions immediately

b) By escalating all issues

c) By minimizing downtime and optimizing functionality

d) By ignoring potential side effects

Answer: c) By minimizing downtime and optimizing functionality

Explanation: The troubleshooting methodology contributes to system reliability by minimizing downtime and optimizing overall functionality through systematic issue resolution.

17. What is the primary purpose of documenting findings in troubleshooting?

a) To confuse users

b) To escalate the issue

c) To verify system functionality

d) To provide a reference for future problem-solving

Answer: d) To provide a reference for future problem-solving

Explanation: Documenting findings in troubleshooting serves as a valuable reference for future problem-solving, enabling efficient and effective issue resolution.

18. Why is it essential to verify full system functionality in troubleshooting?

a) To escalate the issue

b) To document findings

c) To ensure the problem is unresolved

d) To confirm that the issue is resolved and the system functions correctly

Answer: d) To confirm that the issue is resolved and the system functions correctly

Explanation: Verifying full system functionality in troubleshooting ensures that the issue is resolved and the system operates correctly after implementing solutions.

19. What is the role of processing speed in computing?

a) Quantifying data storage capacity

b) Measuring the rate of data transfer

c) Determining the speed at which a computer performs operations

d) Analyzing data and creating information

Answer: c) Determining the speed at which a computer performs operations

Explanation: Processing speed in computing determines how quickly a computer's central processing unit (CPU) performs operations.

20. Which unit of measure is used to quantify data storage capacity in computing?

a) Hertz (Hz)

b) Kilobits per second (kbps)

c) Terabytes

d) Megabytes

Answer: c) Terabytes

Explanation: Terabytes are a unit of measure used to quantify data storage capacity in computing.

21. How does data representation contribute to effective communication between humans and computers?

a) By encrypting data

b) By compressing data

c) By encoding data in machine-readable formats

d) By limiting data access

Answer: c) By encoding data in machine-readable formats

Explanation: Data representation contributes to effective communication by encoding data in machine-readable formats, facilitating interaction between humans and computers.

22. Why is the understanding of notational systems important in information technology?

a) To confuse users

b) To optimize data storage

c) To enhance data encryption

d) To navigate data representation and manipulation

Answer: d) To navigate data representation and manipulation

Explanation: Understanding notational systems is important in information technology to effectively navigate data representation and manipulation, facilitating communication with computing systems.

23. How does the concept of data as an asset relate to its strategic importance?

a) By limiting data access

b) By emphasizing data as a liability

c) By recognizing data's value and significance to individuals, organizations, and society

d) By prioritizing data deletion

Answer: c) By recognizing data's value and significance to individuals, organizations, and society

Explanation: Treating data as an asset involves recognizing its value and significance to individuals, organizations, and society, emphasizing its strategic importance.

24. What is the primary purpose of digital rights management in the context of data and information?

a) To limit data access

b) To enhance data encryption

c) To manage and protect intellectual property

d) To accelerate data processing speed

Answer: c) To manage and protect intellectual property

Explanation: Digital rights management is used to manage and protect intellectual property related to digital data and content.

25. How do data-driven business decisions contribute to a competitive edge?

a) By slowing down business processes

b) By limiting access to data

c) By optimizing operations, enhancing customer experiences, and gaining a competitive edge

d) By ignoring market trends

Answer: c) By optimizing operations, enhancing customer experiences, and gaining a competitive edge

Explanation: Data-driven business decisions contribute to a competitive edge by optimizing operations, enhancing customer experiences, and leveraging data for strategic advantage.

26. What does the troubleshooting methodology prioritize in addressing issues within computing systems?

a) Implementing preventive measures

b) Minimizing downtime and optimizing functionality

c) Documenting findings for future reference

d) Ignoring potential side effects

Answer: b) Minimizing downtime and optimizing functionality

Explanation: The troubleshooting methodology prioritizes minimizing downtime and optimizing overall functionality in addressing issues within computing systems.

27. How does the understanding of common units of measure benefit decision-making in information technology?

a) By confusing users

b) By simplifying data representation

c) By limiting computing capabilities

d) By quantifying and comparing computing resources

Answer: d) By quantifying and comparing computing resources

Explanation: Understanding common units of measure benefits decision-making by quantifying and facilitating the comparison of computing resources.

28. Why is intellectual property protection crucial for fostering creativity and innovation in the digital realm?

a) To limit data access

b) To enhance data encryption

c) To safeguard against cybersecurity threats

d) To provide legal protection and encourage creativity

Answer: d) To provide legal protection and encourage creativity

Explanation: Intellectual property protection provides legal safeguards and encourages creativity and innovation by ensuring that creators are rewarded for their digital inventions.

29. How does data representation differ from data storage in computing?

a) By prioritizing data deletion

b) By encoding data in machine-readable formats

c) By limiting data access

d) By facilitating data retrieval efficiency

Answer: b) By encoding data in machine-readable formats

Explanation: Data representation involves encoding data in machine-readable formats, whereas data storage focuses on preserving data for future retrieval.

30. What is the primary purpose of throughput units in computing?

a) To quantify data storage capacity

b) To measure processing speed

c) To gauge the rate of data transfer

d) To facilitate data compression

Answer: c) To gauge the rate of data transfer

Explanation: Throughput units, such as bits per second, gauge the rate of data transfer in computing systems.

Chapter 2 Infrastructure

In the ever-evolving landscape of information technology, the infrastructure serves as the backbone of computing systems, providing the essential framework for seamless operations. This chapter delves into the classification of common types of input/output device interfaces, the setup and installation of peripheral devices, and the underlying purpose of various internal computing components.

2.1 Classify Common Types of Input/Output Device Interfaces

The efficiency of a computing system often relies on the seamless communication between various input and output devices. Understanding and classifying common types of interfaces is fundamental for ensuring compatibility and optimal functionality.

Networking Interfaces: These interfaces facilitate communication between computers and networks, enabling data exchange. Examples include Ethernet ports and network interface cards (NICs).

Wireless Interfaces: In an era dominated by mobility, wireless interfaces play a crucial role. Wi-Fi and Bluetooth are prominent examples, enabling connectivity without physical cables.

Peripheral Device Interfaces: These interfaces connect external devices to the computer. USB (Universal Serial Bus), Thunderbolt, and HDMI are common interfaces for peripherals like printers, keyboards, and monitors.

Graphic Device Interfaces: Graphics play a vital role in modern computing. Interfaces such as HDMI, DisplayPort, and VGA connect graphic devices like monitors and projectors to display visual information.

Understanding these interfaces is pivotal for configuring systems, ensuring compatibility, and optimizing the user experience.

2.2 Given a Scenario, Set Up and Install Common Peripheral Devices to a Laptop/PC.

The practical aspect of infrastructure involves the setup and installation of peripheral devices, enhancing the functionality of laptops and PCs.

Devices: Peripheral devices encompass a wide range, including printers, scanners, external hard drives, and more. The specific device depends on the user's needs and the computing environment.

Installation Types: Installation methods vary based on the device. USB devices often follow a plug-and-play approach, while others may require driver installations or firmware updates. The installation process ensures that the device is recognized and operates seamlessly with the computer.

Understanding how to set up and install peripheral devices is crucial for users and IT professionals alike, as it directly impacts the usability and versatility of the computing system.

2.3 Explain the Purpose of Common Internal Computing Components

Internal computing components form the core of a computer, contributing to its overall functionality. Understanding the purpose of each component is essential for system comprehension and troubleshooting.

Motherboard/System Board: The motherboard is the central hub connecting all components. It houses the CPU, RAM, GPU, and facilitates communication between them.

Firmware/BIOS: Basic Input/Output System (BIOS) or firmware is responsible for initializing and providing essential communication between hardware components during the system's startup.

RAM (Random Access Memory): RAM is volatile memory that provides temporary storage for data that the CPU is actively using or processing. It allows for quick access, enhancing system performance.

CPU (Central Processing Unit): Often referred to as the brain of the computer, the CPU executes instructions, performs calculations, and manages data flow within the system.

Storage: Storage devices, such as hard drives and SSDs, store data permanently. The operating system, applications, and user files are stored on these devices.

GPU (Graphics Processing Unit): The GPU is dedicated to rendering graphics and is essential for visual-intensive tasks, including gaming, video editing, and graphic design.

Cooling: To prevent overheating, computers employ cooling mechanisms such as fans or liquid cooling systems. These ensure that internal components operate within optimal temperature ranges.

NIC (Network Interface Card): The NIC facilitates communication between the computer and a network, allowing data exchange with other devices.

Understanding the roles and interactions of these internal components is foundational for anyone involved in computer maintenance, troubleshooting, or system customization. It forms the basis for harnessing the full potential of computing infrastructure.

2.4 Compare and Contrast Common Internet Service Types

The availability of various Internet service types allows users to choose the most suitable option based on their needs. Here's a comparison of three common types:

Fiber Optic:

Advantages: High-speed, reliable, and less susceptible to interference.

Disadvantages: Limited availability in some areas, potentially higher cost.

DSL (Digital Subscriber Line):

Advantages: Widespread availability, lower cost compared to fiber optic.

Disadvantages: Speed may vary based on distance from the service provider's central office.

Wireless:

Advantages: Highly flexible, convenient, and often used for mobile devices.

Disadvantages: Speed and reliability may be affected by signal strength and interference.

Understanding these differences allows users to choose an Internet service that aligns with their priorities, whether it's speed, reliability, or cost.

2.5 Compare and Contrast Storage Types

Effective data storage is crucial in computing, and various types serve different purposes:

Volatile vs. Non-Volatile:

Volatile: Loses data when power is turned off (e.g., RAM).

Non-Volatile: Retains data even when power is off (e.g., hard drives, SSDs).

Local Storage Types:

Hard Drives: Higher capacity but slower.

Solid-State Drives (SSDs): Faster but may have less storage capacity.

Local Network Storage Types:

Network-Attached Storage (NAS): Shared storage accessible over a network.

Direct-Attached Storage (DAS): Connected directly to a single computer.

Cloud Storage Service:

Advantages: Accessibility from anywhere, scalability.

Disadvantages: Requires internet access, potential security concerns.

Understanding these distinctions aids users in selecting the right storage solutions for their specific needs.

2.6 Compare and Contrast Common Computing Devices and Their Purposes

Computing devices come in various forms, each designed for specific purposes:

Mobile Phones:

Purpose: Communication, mobile applications, and general utility.

Characteristics: Portable, touchscreen interface.

Tablets:

Purpose: Portable computing and media consumption.

Characteristics: Larger than mobile phones, touchscreen interface.

Laptops:

Purpose: Portable computing with a physical keyboard.

Characteristics: Compact, integrated keyboard, and display.

Workstations:

Purpose: High-performance computing for specialized tasks (e.g., graphic design, video editing).

Characteristics: Powerful processors, ample RAM, dedicated GPUs.

Servers:

Purpose: Provide services to other devices over a network.

Characteristics: Robust hardware, often located in data centers.

Gaming Consoles:

Purpose: Dedicated gaming and entertainment.

Characteristics: Optimized for gaming, often connected to TVs.

IoT (Internet of Things):

Purpose: Embedded computing in everyday objects for connectivity.

Characteristics: Small, specialized, often with minimal user interface.

Understanding the roles of these devices helps users choose the right tool for specific tasks.

2.7 Explain Basic Networking Concepts

Networking forms the foundation of modern communication, involving several key concepts:

Basics of Network Communication:

Data exchange between devices over a network, enabling communication and resource sharing.

Device Addresses:

Devices are identified by unique addresses, such as IP addresses and MAC addresses, ensuring accurate communication.

Basic Protocols:

Protocols (e.g., TCP/IP) define rules for data transmission, ensuring standardized communication across networks.

Network Devices:

Devices such as routers, switches, and hubs manage network traffic and enable connectivity.

Understanding these basic networking concepts is essential for anyone working with computers and interconnected systems.

2.8 Given a Scenario, Install, Configure, and Secure a Basic Wireless Network

Setting up a wireless network involves various considerations to ensure functionality and security:

802.11a/b/g/n/ac:

802.11 Standards: Different versions with varying speeds and compatibility.

Recommendation: Use the latest standard (e.g., 802.11ac) for optimal performance.

Network Devices Best Practices:

Position routers centrally for better coverage.

Secure routers with strong passwords and disable unnecessary features.

WEP, WPA, WPA2:

WEP (Wired Equivalent Privacy): Weak security, easily compromised.

WPA (Wi-Fi Protected Access): Improved security compared to WEP.

WPA2: Stronger encryption, recommended for secure wireless networks.

Understanding these wireless networking components and best practices ensures the successful installation, configuration, and security of a basic wireless network.

Practice Question and Answers on Infrastructure

1. Which type of Internet service is known for its high-speed and reliability, utilizing thin strands of glass to transmit data signals?

a) DSL

b) Wireless

c) Fiber Optic

d) Satellite

Answer: c) Fiber Optic

Explanation: Fiber optic Internet service uses thin strands of glass to transmit data signals, offering high-speed and reliable connectivity.

2. What is a potential disadvantage of DSL Internet service?

a) Limited availability

b) High cost

c) High susceptibility to interference

d) Limited speed

Answer: a) Limited availability

Explanation: DSL Internet service may have limited availability, especially in areas far from the service provider's central office.

3. Which wireless interface is commonly used for connecting mobile devices, such as smartphones and tablets, to the Internet?

a) Wi-Fi

b) Bluetooth

c) NFC (Near Field Communication)

d) Zigbee

Answer: a) Wi-Fi

Explanation: Wi-Fi is commonly used for wireless connectivity in mobile devices like smartphones and tablets.

4. What is a characteristic of volatile storage in computing?

a) Retains data even when power is off

b) Loses data when power is off

c) Has high storage capacity

d) Is resistant to data corruption

Answer: b) Loses data when power is off

Explanation: Volatile storage, like RAM, loses data when power is turned off.

5. What is a key advantage of Cloud Storage Services?

a) Limited accessibility

b) High cost

c) Scalability

d) Low data security

Answer: c) Scalability

Explanation: Cloud Storage Services offer scalability, allowing users to easily adjust their storage needs as required.

6. Which computing device is designed for specialized tasks such as graphic design and video editing, often equipped with powerful processors and dedicated GPUs?

a) Mobile Phones

b) Tablets

c) Workstations

d) Servers

Answer: c) Workstations

Explanation: Workstations are designed for high-performance computing tasks, such as graphic design and video editing.

7. What is the primary purpose of a server in a computing environment?

a) Gaming

b) Providing services to other devices over a network

c) Mobile communication

d) Graphic design

Answer: b) Providing services to other devices over a network

Explanation: Servers are dedicated to providing services to other devices over a network.

8. Which networking concept involves data exchange between devices over a network, enabling communication and resource sharing?

a) Device Addresses

b) Basic Protocols

c) Networking Devices

d) Basics of Network Communication

Answer: d) Basics of Network Communication

Explanation: Basics of Network Communication involve data exchange between devices over a network.

9. What is the purpose of device addresses in networking, such as IP addresses and MAC addresses?

a) To facilitate data encryption

b) To identify devices uniquely and ensure accurate communication

c) To limit network access

d) To determine network speed

Answer: b) To identify devices uniquely and ensure accurate communication

Explanation: Device addresses, such as IP addresses and MAC addresses, are used to identify devices uniquely and ensure accurate communication.

10. Which wireless security protocol is considered the most secure among the options listed?

a) WEP (Wired Equivalent Privacy)

b) WPA (Wi-Fi Protected Access)

c) WPA2

d) None of the above

Answer: c) WPA2

Explanation: WPA2 is considered more secure than WEP and WPA, offering stronger encryption for wireless networks.

11. In the context of Internet services, what does DSL stand for?

a) Digital Signal Line

b) Dynamic Service Link

c) Digital Subscriber Line

d) Direct Satellite Link

Answer: c) Digital Subscriber Line

Explanation: DSL stands for Digital Subscriber Line, a common type of Internet service.

12. Which type of storage is known for retaining data even when the power is turned off and is commonly used for long-term storage of files and applications?

a) Volatile storage

b) Non-volatile storage

c) Cloud storage

d) Network-Attached Storage (NAS)

Answer: b) Non-volatile storage

Explanation: Non-volatile storage retains data even when the power is turned off, making it suitable for long-term storage.

13. What is a characteristic of solid-state drives (SSDs) compared to traditional hard drives?

a) Higher storage capacity

b) Slower data transfer speeds

c) Magnetic storage technology

d) Faster data access speeds

Answer: d) Faster data access speeds

Explanation: Solid-state drives (SSDs) are known for faster data access speeds compared to traditional hard drives.

14. What is the primary purpose of a network-attached storage (NAS) device?

a) Directly attached to a single computer

b) Shared storage accessible over a network

c) Used for portable computing

d) Optimized for gaming

Answer: b) Shared storage accessible over a network

Explanation: Network-Attached Storage (NAS) devices provide shared storage accessible over a network.

15. Which wireless standard is commonly used for connecting devices like laptops, smartphones, and tablets to a home Wi-Fi network?

a) 802.11a

b) 802.11b

c) 802.11g

d) 802.11n

Answer: d) 802.11n

Explanation: 802.11n is a common wireless standard used for connecting devices to home Wi-Fi networks.

16. What is the purpose of a firewall in the context of network security?

a) To enhance data encryption

b) To limit network access

c) To increase network speed

d) To facilitate device communication

Answer: b) To limit network access

Explanation: Firewalls are designed to limit unauthorized access to a network, enhancing security.

17. In the context of computing devices, what is the primary function of RAM (Random Access Memory)?

a) Long-term storage of files

b) Retaining data even when power is off

c) Executing instructions and temporarily storing active data

d) Facilitating network communication

Answer: c) Executing instructions and temporarily storing active data

Explanation: RAM (Random Access Memory) is used for executing instructions and temporarily storing active data during a computer's operation.

18. What is the primary purpose of a GPU (Graphics Processing Unit) in a computing device?

a) Executing instructions

b) Storing data permanently

c) Rendering graphics and images

d) Managing network communication

Answer: c) Rendering graphics and images

Explanation: The primary purpose of a GPU is to render graphics and images, handling visual processing tasks.

19. What is a common use case for Internet of Things (IoT) devices?

a) Graphic design

b) Mobile communication

c) Embedded computing in everyday objects for connectivity

d) Providing services to other devices over a network

Answer: c) Embedded computing in everyday objects for connectivity

Explanation: IoT devices are designed for embedded computing in everyday objects, enabling connectivity and smart functionalities.

20. What is a characteristic of a well-configured wireless network for optimal coverage?

a) Placing routers in isolated corners

b) Positioning routers centrally for better coverage

c) Using weak passwords for security

d) Disabling encryption for faster data transfer

Answer: b) Positioning routers centrally for better coverage

Explanation: Positioning routers centrally helps achieve better coverage in a wireless network.

21. Which networking device is responsible for managing data traffic between devices within a local network?

a) Router

b) Switch

c) Hub

d) Modem

Answer: b) Switch

Explanation: A switch is responsible for managing data traffic between devices within a local network.

22. What is the purpose of the BIOS (Basic Input/Output System) in a computer system?

a) Providing network services

b) Initializing hardware components during startup

c) Executing applications

d) Managing storage devices

Answer: b) Initializing hardware components during startup

Explanation: The BIOS initializes hardware components during a computer's startup process.

23. Which wireless security protocol is considered outdated and insecure, and should be avoided for securing a wireless network?

a) WEP (Wired Equivalent Privacy)

b) WPA (Wi-Fi Protected Access)

c) WPA2

d) WPA3

Answer: a) WEP (Wired Equivalent Privacy)

Explanation: WEP is considered outdated and insecure, and it is recommended to avoid using it for securing a wireless network.

24. What is the primary function of NIC (Network Interface Card) in a computing device?

a) Rendering graphics

b) Executing instructions

c) Managing storage

d) Facilitating network communication

Answer: d) Facilitating network communication

Explanation: The primary function of a Network Interface Card (NIC) is to facilitate network communication in a computing device.

25. Which component is responsible for determining the speed at which a computer performs operations?

a) Storage device

b) CPU (Central Processing Unit)

c) RAM (Random Access Memory)

d) GPU (Graphics Processing Unit)

Answer: b) CPU (Central Processing Unit)

Explanation: The CPU (Central Processing Unit) is responsible for determining the speed at which a computer performs operations.

26. What is the purpose of a cooling system in a computing device?

a) Enhancing data encryption

b) Minimizing downtime and optimizing functionality

c) Preventing overheating of internal components

d) Facilitating network communication

Answer: c) Preventing overheating of internal components

Explanation: The cooling system in a computing device is designed to prevent overheating of internal components, ensuring optimal performance.

27. What is the primary focus of troubleshooting in the context of computing systems?

a) Implementing preventive measures

b) Minimizing downtime and optimizing functionality

c) Documenting findings for future reference

d) Ignoring potential side effects

Answer: b) Minimizing downtime and optimizing functionality

Explanation: The primary focus of troubleshooting is minimizing downtime and optimizing functionality within computing systems.

28. Why is it important to secure a wireless network with strong authentication and encryption protocols?

a) To limit network access

b) To increase network speed

c) To enhance data encryption

d) To prevent unauthorized access and protect data

Answer: d) To prevent unauthorized access and protect data

Explanation: Securing a wireless network with strong authentication and encryption protocols is crucial to prevent unauthorized access and protect data.

29. What is the purpose of documenting findings in troubleshooting?

a) To confuse users

b) To escalate the issue

c) To verify system functionality

d) To provide a reference for future problem-solving

Answer: d) To provide a reference for future problem-solving

Explanation: Documenting findings in troubleshooting serves as a reference for future problem-solving, facilitating efficient issue resolution.

30. In the context of storage units, what does the term "terabytes" refer to?

a) Rate of data transfer

b) Data storage capacity

c) Processing speed

d) Throughput unit

Answer: b) Data storage capacity

Explanation: Terabytes refer to data storage capacity in storage units, indicating the amount of data that can be stored.

Chapter 3. Applications and Software

In the dynamic landscape of information technology, the role of operating systems (OS) is paramount. This chapter explores the fundamental purpose of operating systems, delving into their crucial functionalities and various types.

3.1 Explain the Purpose of Operating Systems

Interface Between Applications and Hardware:

Operating systems serve as a bridge, providing a user-friendly interface between applications and the underlying hardware. This interface allows users and applications to interact with hardware resources without dealing with intricate details.

Disk Management:

Operating systems oversee disk management, ensuring efficient storage and retrieval of data. This includes organizing files, managing disk space, and facilitating data storage optimization.

Process Management/Scheduling:

Efficient process management is a key responsibility of an operating system. It involves task scheduling, ensuring that multiple processes run seamlessly, and allocating system resources to optimize performance.

Application Management:

Operating systems handle application management by facilitating the execution of software programs. They provide an environment in which applications can run, managing their lifecycle from start to finish.

Memory Management:

Operating systems manage system memory, allocating and deallocating memory space for applications. This ensures that each running application has access to the required memory resources.

Device Management:

Operating systems coordinate with various hardware devices, managing their communication with the computer. This includes input and output devices, ensuring seamless interaction between the computer and peripherals.

Access Control/Protection:

Operating systems implement access control mechanisms to protect data and resources from unauthorized access. This involves user authentication, permissions, and encryption to secure sensitive information.

Types of OS:

There are several types of operating systems, each designed for specific purposes. Examples include:

Single-User, Single-Tasking OS: Designed for individual users and supports only one task at a time.

Single-User, Multi-Tasking OS: Allows a single user to run multiple applications simultaneously.

Multi-User OS: Supports multiple users accessing the system concurrently, often in a networked environment.

Real-Time OS: Designed for systems that require immediate processing and response, common in embedded systems and critical applications.

Understanding the purpose and functionalities of operating systems is essential for users, administrators, and developers to harness the full potential of computing resources.

3.2 Compare and Contrast Components of an Operating System

An operating system is a complex software that comprises various components working together to provide a seamless computing experience. Let's explore and compare the key components of an operating system:

File Systems and Features:

File Systems:

Definition: File systems manage how data is stored, organized, and retrieved on storage devices.

Examples: NTFS (New Technology File System), FAT32 (File Allocation Table), ext4 (Fourth Extended File System).

Features:

Definition: Features enhance the capabilities of the operating system, providing additional functionalities.

Examples: Multitasking, multiuser support, graphical user interface (GUI), security features.

File Management:

Definition: File management involves organizing, storing, and retrieving files on storage devices.

Responsibilities: Creating, deleting, renaming, and organizing files and directories.

Services:

Definition: Services are background processes that run independently and provide specific functionalities.

Examples: Print spooler service, network services, security services.

Processes:

Definition: Processes are running instances of programs, representing the execution of tasks.

Responsibilities: Managing processes involves scheduling, multitasking, and resource allocation.

Drivers:

Definition: Drivers are software components that allow the operating system to communicate with hardware devices.

Responsibilities: Providing a standardized interface for hardware peripherals.

Utilities:

Definition: Utilities are specialized tools that perform specific tasks related to system management.

Examples: Disk cleanup, antivirus utilities, backup tools.

Interfaces:

Definition: Interfaces act as a means for users and applications to interact with the operating system.

Types: Command-line interfaces (CLI), graphical user interfaces (GUI), touch-based interfaces.

Comparison:

File Systems vs. File Management: File systems define how data is stored, while file management involves day-to-day organization and manipulation of files.

Services vs. Processes: Services are background tasks that run independently, while processes are running instances of programs actively performing tasks.

Drivers vs. Utilities: Drivers enable communication with hardware, while utilities are tools that perform various system management tasks.

Interfaces vs. Features: Interfaces provide a user-friendly way to interact with the system, while features enhance the overall capabilities of the operating system.

Understanding the roles and interactions of these components is crucial for users, administrators, and developers to effectively utilize and maintain an operating system. Each component plays a distinct role in ensuring the smooth functioning of the entire system.

3.3 Purpose and Proper Use of Software

Software plays a pivotal role in enhancing productivity, enabling collaboration, and supporting various business functions. Understanding the purpose and proper use of different categories of software is essential for maximizing their benefits.

Productivity Software:

Purpose:

Productivity software is designed to aid individuals and organizations in completing tasks efficiently, managing information, and enhancing overall productivity.

Proper Use:

Word Processing Software: Use for creating, editing, and formatting text documents.

Spreadsheets: Ideal for data analysis, financial modeling, and organization of numerical information.

Presentation Software: Utilize for creating visual presentations with slides, graphics, and multimedia elements.

Note-Taking Apps: Useful for capturing ideas, notes, and organizing information.

Collaboration Software:

Purpose:

Collaboration software focuses on facilitating communication and teamwork among individuals or groups, often in different locations.

Proper Use:

Email and Messaging Apps: Effective for quick communication and sharing of information.

Project Management Tools: Use for planning, organizing, and tracking progress on projects.

Document Collaboration Platforms: Enable multiple users to work on the same document simultaneously.

Virtual Meeting Software: Facilitate online meetings, video conferences, and collaborative discussions.

Business Software:

Purpose:

Business software is tailored to meet the specific needs of organizations, addressing functions such as accounting, customer relationship management (CRM), and enterprise resource planning (ERP).

Proper Use:

Accounting Software: Essential for managing financial transactions, budgeting, and generating financial reports.

CRM Software: Aids in managing customer interactions, tracking leads, and maintaining customer relationships.

ERP Systems: Integrates various business processes, streamlining operations across departments.

Human Resource Management (HRM) Software: Manages employee information, payroll, and HR processes.

Guidelines for Proper Software Use:

Compatibility: Ensure that the software is compatible with the operating system and hardware.

Licensing and Compliance: Adhere to licensing agreements and comply with software usage policies.

Training and Support: Provide adequate training to users and access to support resources.

Security: Implement security measures to protect sensitive data and prevent unauthorized access.

Regular Updates: Keep software up to date with the latest patches and updates to ensure optimal performance and security.

Customization: Explore customization options to tailor the software to specific organizational needs.

By understanding the purpose and following proper usage guidelines, individuals and organizations can harness the full potential of software to enhance productivity, collaboration, and overall business efficiency.

3.4 Methods of Application Architecture and Delivery Models

The methods of application architecture and delivery models play a crucial role in how software applications are designed, deployed, and accessed. Understanding these methods is essential for making informed decisions about application development and deployment strategies.

Application Delivery Methods:

**1. Locally Installed Applications:

Definition: Locally installed applications are software programs that are downloaded and installed on individual computers or devices.

Characteristics:

Run directly on the user's device.

Require manual installation and periodic updates.

Accessible without continuous internet connectivity.

2. Cloud Hosted Applications:

Definition: Cloud hosted applications, or cloud applications, are software programs that run on remote servers and are accessed through the internet.

Characteristics:

Hosted on cloud infrastructure.

Accessible from various devices with an internet connection.

Updates and maintenance are managed centrally.

Application Architecture Models:

**1. Monolithic Architecture:

Definition: In a monolithic architecture, the entire application is designed and deployed as a single, tightly integrated unit.

Characteristics:

Single codebase.

All components share the same database.

Scaling can be challenging.

2. Microservices Architecture:

Definition: Microservices architecture breaks down an application into small, independent services that communicate with each other through APIs.

Characteristics:

Independent development and deployment of services.

Each service has its own database.

Easier scalability and maintenance.

3. Client-Server Architecture:

Definition: In client-server architecture, the application is split into two parts – the client (user interface) and the server (database and processing logic).

Characteristics:

Client sends requests to the server for processing.

Centralized data management on the server.

Common in web applications.

4. Distributed Architecture:

Definition: Distributed architecture involves components running on different machines that communicate and coordinate to achieve a common goal.

Characteristics:

Decentralized processing and data storage.

Improved fault tolerance and scalability.

Guidelines for Choosing Delivery Models and Architecture:

Scalability: Consider the scalability requirements of the application. Cloud-hosted and microservices architectures are often more scalable.

Flexibility: Choose an architecture that provides flexibility in development, deployment, and maintenance. Microservices offer greater flexibility in this regard.

Cost: Evaluate the cost implications of hosting and maintaining applications. Cloud hosting may offer cost-effective solutions.

Performance: Assess the performance requirements of the application. Certain architectures may be better suited for high-performance applications.

Uscr Accessibility: Consider how users will access the application. Locally installed applications may be suitable for offline use, while cloud-hosted applications provide accessibility from anywhere.

Development Team Expertise: Assess the expertise of the development team. Some architectures may require specialized skills.

By carefully considering these factors, organizations can make informed decisions regarding application delivery methods and architecture models, aligning with their specific requirements and objectives.

3.5 Configuring and Using Web Browsers: Scenario-Based Guidelines

In various scenarios, the configuration of web browsers becomes essential to ensure optimal performance, security, and functionality. Here are guidelines for configuring and using web browsers in specific scenarios:

1. Caching/Clearing Cache:

Scenario: Web pages are not loading properly, or you want to ensure you are viewing the latest content.

Guidelines:

Clear Cache: Navigate to browser settings and clear the cache. This ensures that the browser fetches the latest versions of web pages and resources.

2. Deactivate Client-Side Scripting:

Scenario: Security concerns or specific website compatibility issues.

Guidelines:

Disable JavaScript: Access browser settings and disable client-side scripting (JavaScript) if security concerns arise or if a website doesn't function correctly.

3. Browser Add-ons/Extensions:

Scenario: Enhancing browser functionality with specific features or utilities.

Guidelines:

Install/Add Extensions: Explore browser extension stores (e.g., Chrome Web Store, Firefox Add-ons) to find and install add-ons/extensions that enhance features or provide utility.

4. Private Browsing:

Scenario: When you want to browse without saving history or cookies.

Guidelines:

Activate Private Browsing: Use the browser's private or incognito mode to browse without storing history, passwords, or other session data.

5. Proxy Settings:

Scenario: Accessing the internet through a proxy server for anonymity or network requirements.

Guidelines:

Configure Proxy Settings: In browser settings, configure proxy settings to route internet traffic through a proxy server. Useful for privacy or accessing restricted content.

6. Certificates:

Scenario: Accessing secure websites or resolving certificate-related errors.

Guidelines:

Install/Update Certificates: Ensure that your browser has the necessary root certificates installed. Update certificates if you encounter security warnings on secure websites.

7. Popup Blockers:

Scenario: Preventing unwanted pop-up ads or windows.

Guidelines:

Activate Popup Blocker: Enable the built-in popup blocker in browser settings to prevent annoying and potentially malicious pop-ups.

8. Script Blockers:

Scenario: Enhancing security by preventing the execution of certain scripts.

Guidelines:

Use Script Blocking Extensions: Install browser extensions that allow you to selectively block or enable scripts on specific websites for enhanced security.

9. Compatible Browser for Applications:

Scenario: Using web applications that may have specific browser requirements.

Guidelines:

Check Application Requirements: Verify the recommended or supported browsers for the specific web application. Use the recommended browser for optimal compatibility.

By configuring web browsers based on these scenarios, users can customize their browsing experience, enhance security, and ensure compatibility with various web applications and content.

3.6 Comparing and Contrasting General Application Concepts and Uses

Understanding general application concepts and their uses is crucial for making informed decisions about software selection, deployment, and management. Let's compare and contrast key concepts in the realm of applications:

1. Single-Platform Software:

Definition: Single-platform software is designed to run exclusively on a specific operating system or hardware platform.

Characteristics:

Limited Compatibility: Only works on the designated platform.

Optimized Performance: Can be optimized for the specific features and capabilities of the platform.

Easier Development: Development efforts can be focused on a single platform.

2. Cross-Platform Software:

Definition: Cross-platform software is developed to run on multiple operating systems or hardware platforms.

Characteristics:

Broad Compatibility: Compatible with different operating systems or platforms.

Increased Development Effort: Development requires addressing variations in platform-specific features.

Enhanced Reach: Appeals to a wider audience using diverse devices.

3. Licensing:

Definition: Licensing refers to the legal permissions and restrictions governing the use, distribution, and modification of software.

Characteristics:

Ownership Rights: Dictates user rights, including usage, distribution, and modification privileges.

Types: Licensing models vary, including proprietary, open-source, freeware, and shareware.

Compliance: Users must adhere to licensing terms to use the software legally.

4. Software Installation Best Practices:

Guidelines:

Source Reliability: Download software from official sources or trusted repositories to avoid malware or security risks.

Check System Requirements: Ensure compatibility with your operating system and hardware.

Read User Agreement: Understand licensing terms and conditions before installation.

Update and Patch: Regularly update software to benefit from improvements, bug fixes, and security patches.

Custom Installation: Opt for custom installations to select specific features and avoid bloatware.

Comparison and Contrast:

Single-Platform vs. Cross-Platform Software:

Single-Platform: Limited to a specific platform, optimized for performance on that platform.

Cross-Platform: Offers broad compatibility, addressing the challenges of diverse platforms but may require more development effort.

Licensing vs. Software Installation Best Practices:

Licensing: Governs legal use and distribution; adherence is crucial for compliance.

Installation Best Practices: Focus on ensuring secure, reliable, and compliant software installation.

Understanding these concepts allows users, developers, and decision-makers to navigate the landscape of software applications effectively. Whether choosing between single-platform and cross-platform solutions or ensuring compliance through proper licensing and installation practices, a clear understanding of these concepts is vital for making informed decisions.

Practice Questions and Answers on Applications and Software

1. What is the primary purpose of productivity software?

a) Entertainment

b) Enhancing system security

c) Managing financial transactions

d) Completing tasks efficiently

Answer: d) Completing tasks efficiently

2. Which type of software allows multiple users to work on the same document simultaneously?

a) Spreadsheet software

b) Presentation software

c) Document collaboration platform

d) Note-taking app

Answer: c) Document collaboration platform

3. In the context of collaboration software, what does CRM stand for?

a) Customer Relationship Management

b) Centralized Resource Management

c) Creative Resource Model

d) Communication and Relationship Module

Answer: a) Customer Relationship Management

4. What is the purpose of cloud-hosted applications?

a) Run exclusively on a single device

b) Accessed through the internet from remote servers

c) Installed locally on every user's device

d) Designed for offline use only

Answer: b) Accessed through the internet from remote servers

5. In application architecture, what does the microservices model involve?

a) Integration of all components into a single unit

b) Breaking down an application into small, independent services

c) Centralized processing and data storage

d) Single, tightly integrated codebase

Answer: b) Breaking down an application into small, independent services

6. What is the primary purpose of a popup blocker in a web browser?

a) Enhancing security

b) Allowing pop-ups for every website

c) Facilitating communication between websites

d) Preventing unwanted pop-up ads or windows

Answer: d) Preventing unwanted pop-up ads or windows

7. How can you enhance security by preventing the execution of certain scripts in a web browser?

a) Activate private browsing

b) Install popup blockers

c) Use script blocking extensions

d) Clear browser cache

Answer: c) Use script blocking extensions

8. What is the purpose of clearing the cache in a web browser?

a) Improving system performance

b) Preventing unauthorized access

c) Enhancing security

d) Fetching the latest versions of web pages and resources

Answer: d) Fetching the latest versions of web pages and resources

9. When configuring proxy settings in a web browser, what does it allow you to do?

a) Optimize performance

b) Route internet traffic through a proxy server

c) Disable browser extensions

d) Activate private browsing

Answer: b) Route internet traffic through a proxy server

10. What is the purpose of certificates in web browsers?

a) Managing financial transactions

b) Enhancing system security

c) Routing internet traffic

d) Establishing secure connections with websites

Answer: d) Establishing secure connections with websites

11. What does cross-platform software provide in terms of compatibility?

a) Limited compatibility with specific platforms

b) Broad compatibility across different operating systems or platforms

c) Compatibility only with Windows

d) Compatibility exclusively with mobile devices

Answer: b) Broad compatibility across different operating systems or platforms

12. What is the primary factor that influences the development of single-platform software?

a) Enhanced reach

b) Broad compatibility

c) Limited compatibility

d) Increased development effort

Answer: c) Limited compatibility

13. In licensing, what does adherence to terms and conditions ensure?

a) Optimal performance

b) Legal use and distribution

c) Compatibility with various platforms

d) Enhanced security features

Answer: b) Legal use and distribution

14. What is a best practice for software installation to avoid security risks?

a) Download software from official sources or trusted repositories

b) Install software without checking system requirements

c) Ignore user agreements during installation

d) Use outdated versions of software

Answer: a) Download software from official sources or trusted repositories

15. Which architecture model involves breaking down an application into small, independent services?

a) Monolithic architecture

b) Microservices architecture

c) Client-server architecture

d) Distributed architecture

Answer: b) Microservices architecture

16. What type of software is designed for offline use and accessed through a single device only?

a) Cross-platform software

b) Cloud-hosted software

c) Single-platform software

d) Collaboration software

Answer: c) Single-platform software

17. What does a document collaboration platform enable users to do?

a) Run multiple applications simultaneously

b) Work on the same document simultaneously

c) Manage customer relationships

d) Optimize system performance

Answer: b) Work on the same document simultaneously

18. In web browsers, what is the purpose of private browsing mode?

a) Facilitating communication between websites

b) Browsing without saving history or cookies

c) Blocking unwanted pop-ups

d) Preventing the execution of certain scripts

Answer: b) Browsing without saving history or cookies

19. Which type of architecture involves the entire application as a single, tightly integrated unit?

a) Microservices architecture

b) Distributed architecture

c) Monolithic architecture

d) Client-server architecture

Answer: c) Monolithic architecture

20. What is the primary focus of CRM software?

a) Enhancing system security

b) Managing customer relationships

c) Breaking down applications into services

d) Facilitating communication between users

Answer: b) Managing customer relationships

21. How can users enhance security by preventing unwanted pop-up ads in web browsers?

a) Clearing browser cache

b) Activating private browsing mode

c) Installing popup blockers

d) Disabling JavaScript

Answer: c) Installing popup blockers

22. What is the primary purpose of cloud-hosted applications?

a) Run exclusively on a single device

b) Accessed through the internet from remote servers

c) Installed locally on every user's device

d) Designed for offline use only

Answer: b) Accessed through the internet from remote servers

23. In software licensing, what does adherence to terms and conditions ensure?

a) Enhanced reach

b) Legal use and distribution

c) Broad compatibility

d) Optimal performance

Answer: b) Legal use and distribution

24. Why is it important to disable client-side scripting in certain scenarios?

a) To improve system performance

b) To prevent unwanted pop-up ads

c) For website compatibility or security concerns

d) To optimize application development

Answer: c) For website compatibility or security concerns

25. What should users check before installing software to ensure compatibility?

a) Read user agreement

b) Clear browser cache

c) Check system requirements

d) Install from untrusted sources

Answer: c) Check system requirements

26. What is the primary responsibility of a document collaboration platform?

a) Managing financial transactions

b) Enhancing system security

c) Organizing files and directories

d) Allowing multiple users to work on the same document

Answer: d) Allowing multiple users to work on the same document

27. Why is it crucial to configure proxy settings in a web browser in certain scenarios?

a) To route internet traffic through a proxy server for anonymity

b) To disable browser extensions

c) To activate private browsing mode

d) To improve system performance

Answer: a) To route internet traffic through a proxy server for anonymity

28. What does a popup blocker in a web browser prevent?

a) Preventing unwanted pop-up ads or windows

b) Enhancing system security

c) Facilitating communication between websites

d) Improving system performance

Answer: a) Preventing unwanted pop-up ads or windows

29. What is the primary purpose of a document collaboration platform?

a) Managing customer relationships

b) Improving system performance

c) Organizing files and directories

d) Allowing multiple users to work on the same document

Answer: d) Allowing multiple users to work on the same document

30. In web browsers, what is the purpose of private browsing mode?

a) Facilitating communication between websites

b) Browsing without saving history or cookies

c) Blocking unwanted pop-ups

d) Preventing the execution of certain scripts

Answer: b) Browsing without saving history or cookies

Chapter 4 Software Development Concepts: Programming Language Categories

In the vast landscape of software development, the choice of programming language is a critical decision that significantly influences the development process and the resulting software product. Programming languages can be categorized into different types based on how they are executed and processed. This section explores and contrasts four prominent categories: Interpreted Languages, Compiled Languages, Query Languages, and Assembly Language.

4.1 Compare and Contrast Programming Language Categories

Interpreted Programming Languages:

Interpreted languages are executed line by line by an interpreter at runtime. These languages, such as Python, JavaScript, and Ruby, are known for their portability and ease of debugging. The source code is directly executed without the need for a separate compilation step. This flexibility allows developers to make quick changes and see immediate results, making interpreted languages conducive to rapid prototyping and development.

However, the runtime interpretation can lead to slower execution speeds compared to compiled languages. Each time the code is run, the interpreter analyzes and executes it, which can introduce a performance overhead. Despite this, the advantages in terms of development speed and portability often make interpreted languages a preferred choice for scripting, web development, and other scenarios where rapid development is crucial.

Compiled Programming Languages:

In contrast, compiled languages involve a separate compilation step before execution. Languages like C, C++, and Java are compiled into machine code or an intermediate bytecode that is executed by the target platform. Compilation translates the entire source code into a format that is optimized for the specific architecture, resulting in faster and more efficient execution.

The compilation step, however, introduces an additional layer of complexity. Developers need to compile the code before running it, and the compiled binary may not be as portable as interpreted code. Yet, the performance gains often make compiled languages preferable for resource-intensive applications, system-level programming, and scenarios where speed is paramount.

Query Languages:

Query languages are specialized languages designed for database interactions. SQL (Structured Query Language) is a prime example. Unlike general-purpose programming languages, query languages focus on retrieving, manipulating, and managing data stored in databases. SQL queries are declarative and express the desired outcome, allowing the database system to determine the most efficient execution plan.

The strength of query languages lies in their ability to handle complex data operations without extensive programming knowledge. Developers can issue queries to extract, filter, and transform data without the need for low-level programming constructs. This makes query languages essential for database-driven applications and data analysis.

Assembly Language:

Assembly language is a low-level programming language that corresponds closely to machine code instructions. It is specific to the architecture of the target processor. Unlike high-level languages, which abstract away hardware details, assembly language provides a direct representation of the processor's instruction set.

Writing code in assembly allows for precise control over hardware resources, making it suitable for tasks such as device drivers, embedded systems, and performance-critical applications. However, it comes at the cost of increased complexity and reduced portability. Assembly language programming requires a deep understanding of the underlying hardware, and the same code may not run on different architectures without modification.

The choice of programming language significantly impacts the software development process. Interpreted languages offer rapid development and portability, compiled languages prioritize performance, query languages specialize in database interactions, and assembly language provides low-level control over hardware. The selection depends on the specific requirements of the project, considering factors such as performance, development speed, and the nature of the application. A comprehensive understanding of these programming language categories empowers developers to make informed decisions based on the goals and constraints of their projects.

4.2 Programming Organizational Techniques and Logic Components

In the realm of software development, effective organization and logical structuring of code are paramount for creating maintainable, scalable, and comprehensible programs. This section explores programming organizational techniques and logic components, emphasizing their role in enhancing code quality and readability.

Programming Organizational Techniques:

Modularization:

Definition: Modularization involves breaking down a program into smaller, independent modules or functions. Each module handles a specific task, promoting code reusability and maintainability.

Benefits: Enhances readability, simplifies debugging, and allows for incremental development and testing.

Code Comments:

Definition: Comments are annotations within the code that provide explanatory information. They don't affect the program's execution but offer insights into the code's purpose, functionality, and usage.

Benefits: Improves code documentation, facilitates collaboration, and aids in understanding complex or intricate sections of code.

Indentation and Formatting:

Definition: Consistent indentation and formatting make the code visually appealing and easy to read. Proper indentation helps convey the logical structure of the code.

Benefits: Enhances code readability, reduces syntax errors, and contributes to a professional and organized appearance.

Naming Conventions:

Definition: Establishing consistent naming conventions for variables, functions, and classes promotes clarity and consistency across the codebase.

Benefits: Improves code readability, makes code self-documenting, and eases collaboration among developers.

Logic Components:

Conditional Statements:

Definition: Conditional statements (e.g., if, else if, else) introduce decision-making in code based on certain conditions. They direct the flow of execution to different branches depending on the evaluation of these conditions.

Use Case: In scenarios where different actions need to be taken based on specific conditions, such as validating user input or handling edge cases.

Loops:

Definition: Loops (e.g., for, while) enable the repeated execution of a block of code. They are instrumental for performing iterative tasks and processing collections of data.

Use Case: When there is a need to perform the same set of operations multiple times, like iterating through an array or processing a sequence of inputs.

Functions/Methods:

Definition: Functions or methods encapsulate a set of instructions, making them reusable units of code. They promote modularization and allow for code abstraction.

Use Case: When a specific task needs to be performed multiple times, isolating that functionality into a function enhances code organization and maintainability.

Error Handling:

Definition: Error handling components (e.g., try-catch blocks) manage exceptions and errors that may occur during the execution of code. They prevent abrupt program termination and provide graceful handling of unexpected situations.

Use Case: In situations where external factors or input variations may lead to errors, implementing error-handling mechanisms ensures robust and resilient code.

Programming organizational techniques and logic components are foundational aspects of creating well-structured and readable code. By employing modularization, commenting, proper indentation, and naming conventions, developers enhance code maintainability and collaboration. Logic components such as conditional statements, loops, functions, and error handling contribute to the logical flow and functionality of the program. A comprehensive understanding and thoughtful application of these techniques result in codebases that are not only functional but also maintainable and adaptable over time.

4.3 Programming Concepts: Identifiers, Containers, Functions, Objects

In the realm of programming, understanding fundamental concepts is crucial for effective code development and organization. This section delves into the purpose and use of four key programming concepts: Identifiers, Containers, Functions, and Objects.

Identifiers:

Purpose:

Identifiers are names given to entities in a program, such as variables, functions, classes, or objects. They serve as labels that allow developers to reference and manipulate these entities in the code. Identifiers play a vital role in making code readable and understandable by providing meaningful names to various elements within the program.

Use:

Variable Naming: Identifiers are extensively used for naming variables, making it clear what information the variable holds.

Function Naming: Functions are identified by their names, indicating their purpose or the task they perform.

Class and Object Naming: In object-oriented programming, identifiers are crucial for naming classes and objects, aiding in code organization.

Example:

python

Copy code

```python
# Identifiers in Python

user_name = "John"

def calculate_total(price, quantity):
    return price * quantity

class Circle:
    def __init__(self, radius):
```

        self.radius = radius

Containers:

Purpose:

Containers, or data structures, are used to store and organize data within a program. They provide a way to group related information, making it easier to manage and manipulate data. Containers play a pivotal role in optimizing data access and retrieval.

Use:

Lists and Arrays: Containers like lists or arrays store sequences of elements.

Dictionaries and Maps: Associative containers like dictionaries store key-value pairs for efficient data retrieval.

Sets: Containers like sets store unique elements without duplicates.

Example:

python

Copy code

```python
# Containers in Python

numbers = [1, 2, 3, 4, 5]  # List

person_info = {"name": "Alice", "age": 25, "city": "XYZ"}  # Dictionary

unique_numbers = {1, 2, 3, 4, 5}  # Set
```

Functions:

Purpose:

Functions are blocks of code that perform a specific task or set of tasks. They promote code reusability, modularization, and abstraction by encapsulating functionality within a named unit. Functions are crucial for structuring code and making it more maintainable.

Use:

Code Abstraction: Functions allow developers to hide the details of a specific task, providing a higher-level abstraction.

Code Reusability: Functions can be reused in multiple parts of a program, reducing redundancy.

Modularization: Breaking down a program into functions facilitates modular development and testing.

Example:

python

Copy code

```python
# Functions in Python

def greet(name):
    return f"Hello, {name}!"

def calculate_area(radius):
    return 3.14 * radius**2
```

Objects:

Purpose:

Objects are instances of classes in object-oriented programming (OOP). They encapsulate data and behavior, providing a way to model real-world entities. Objects facilitate code organization, abstraction, and encapsulation.

Use:

Encapsulation: Objects encapsulate data (attributes) and methods (functions) that operate on that data.

Code Organization: Objects help organize code by grouping related functionality and data.

Inheritance and Polymorphism: Objects support concepts like inheritance, allowing the creation of hierarchies and promoting polymorphic behavior.

Example:

python

Copy code

```python
# Objects in Python

class Car:

    def __init__(self, make, model):

        self.make = make

        self.model = model

    def start_engine(self):

        print(f"The {self.make} {self.model} is starting.")

# Creating an object

my_car = Car("Toyota", "Camry")

# Accessing attributes and invoking methods

print(my_car.make)  # Output: Toyota

my_car.start_engine()  # Output: The Toyota Camry is starting.
```

Identifiers, Containers, Functions, and Objects are foundational concepts that underpin effective programming. Identifiers provide names for elements, Containers organize and store data, Functions encapsulate tasks, and Objects model entities with data and behavior. A deep understanding and adept application of these concepts empower developers to write structured, maintainable, and efficient code.

Practice Question and Answers

1. What is the purpose of identifiers in programming?

a) Enhance code execution speed

b) Provide names to entities in the code

c) Manage errors and exceptions

d) Control program flow

Answer: b) Provide names to entities in the code

Explanation: Identifiers in programming serve as names for variables, functions, classes, or objects. They make code more readable and provide a means of referencing and manipulating different elements within the program.

2. Why are containers important in programming?

a) Enhance code execution speed

b) Provide a way to group and organize data

c) Control program flow

d) Manage errors and exceptions

Answer: b) Provide a way to group and organize data

Explanation: Containers, or data structures, help in organizing and storing data within a program. They are crucial for grouping related information and optimizing data access.

3. What is the primary purpose of functions in programming?

a) Enhance code execution speed

b) Provide names to entities in the code

c) Encapsulate code logic and promote reusability

d) Control program flow

Answer: c) Encapsulate code logic and promote reusability

Explanation: Functions encapsulate code logic, allowing for code abstraction, reusability, and modularization. They make the code more maintainable and readable.

4. In object-oriented programming, what do objects encapsulate?

a) Only data

b) Only code logic

c) Both data and code logic

d) Control program flow

Answer: c) Both data and code logic

Explanation: Objects encapsulate both data (attributes) and code logic (methods) in object-oriented programming, providing a way to model real-world entities.

5. How do containers contribute to efficient data retrieval?

a) By providing names to entities

b) By encapsulating code logic

c) By grouping and organizing data

d) By controlling program flow

Answer: c) By grouping and organizing data

Explanation: Containers, such as lists, dictionaries, and sets, group and organize data, making it easier to manage and retrieve specific pieces of information efficiently.

6. What is the purpose of code comments in programming?

a) Enhance code execution speed

b) Provide a way to group and organize data

c) Facilitate collaboration and improve code documentation

d) Control program flow

Answer: c) Facilitate collaboration and improve code documentation

Explanation: Code comments provide explanatory information within the code, improving collaboration among developers and enhancing code documentation.

7. Why is proper indentation and formatting important in programming?

a) Enhance code execution speed

b) Provide a way to group and organize data

c) Improve code readability and convey logical structure

d) Control program flow

Answer: c) Improve code readability and convey logical structure

Explanation: Proper indentation and formatting make the code visually appealing and easy to read, helping convey the logical structure of the code.

8. What is the primary benefit of using functions in programming?

a) Enhance code execution speed

b) Encapsulate code logic and promote reusability

c) Provide names to entities in the code

d) Control program flow

Answer: b) Encapsulate code logic and promote reusability

Explanation: Functions encapsulate code logic, allowing for code reuse, modularization, and abstraction, contributing to improved code quality.

9. How do objects contribute to code organization in object-oriented programming?

a) By providing names to entities

b) By encapsulating code logic

c) By grouping and organizing data

d) By controlling program flow

Answer: c) By grouping and organizing data

Explanation: Objects group data and code logic related to a specific entity, facilitating code organization and modular development in object-oriented programming.

10. What does modularization involve in programming?

a) Providing names to entities

b) Encapsulating code logic and promoting reusability

c) Breaking down a program into smaller, independent modules

d) Controlling program flow

Answer: c) Breaking down a program into smaller, independent modules

Explanation: Modularization involves breaking down a program into smaller, independent modules or functions, promoting code reusability and maintainability.

11. How do conditional statements contribute to program flow?

a) By providing names to entities

b) By encapsulating code logic

c) By controlling program flow based on conditions

d) By grouping and organizing data

Answer: c) By controlling program flow based on conditions

Explanation: Conditional statements (e.g., if, else) control program flow by directing the execution to different branches based on specified conditions.

12. What is the purpose of error handling components in programming?

a) Enhancing code execution speed

b) Providing a way to group and organize data

c) Managing errors and exceptions that may occur during execution

d) Controlling program flow

Answer: c) Managing errors and exceptions that may occur during execution

Explanation: Error handling components, such as try-catch blocks, manage errors and exceptions, preventing abrupt program termination and providing graceful handling of unexpected situations.

13. How do naming conventions contribute to code readability?

a) By enhancing code execution speed

b) By providing a way to group and organize data

c) By improving code documentation and making code self-explanatory

d) By controlling program flow

Answer: c) By improving code documentation and making code self-explanatory

Explanation: Naming conventions improve code readability by providing consistent and meaningful names to variables, functions, and other entities, making the code self-explanatory.

14. Why are functions essential for code abstraction?

a) To enhance code execution speed

b) To provide a way to group and organize data

c) To encapsulate code logic and hide implementation details

d) To control program flow

Answer: c) To encapsulate code logic and hide implementation details

Explanation: Functions encapsulate code logic, abstracting away implementation details and providing a higher-level view of the functionality they perform.

15. In programming, what does inheritance enable in object-oriented programming?

a) Encapsulation of code logic

b) Code abstraction and reusability

c) Grouping and organizing data

d) Creating hierarchies and promoting polymorphic behavior

Answer: d) Creating hierarchies and promoting polymorphic behavior

Explanation: Inheritance in object-oriented programming allows the creation of class hierarchies, promoting polymorphic behavior and code reuse.

16. How does encapsulation contribute to code maintainability?

a) By enhancing code execution speed

b) By providing names to entities

c) By grouping and organizing data

d) By hiding implementation details and preventing unintended access to data

Answer: d) By hiding implementation details and preventing unintended access to data

Explanation: Encapsulation hides implementation details, allowing changes to be made within the encapsulated unit without affecting other parts of the code and preventing unintended access to data.

17. What is the primary role of objects in object-oriented programming?

a) Enhancing code execution speed

b) Encapsulating code logic and promoting reusability

c) Providing names to entities in the code

d) Controlling program flow

Answer: b) Encapsulating code logic and promoting reusability

Explanation: Objects in object-oriented programming encapsulate both data and code logic related to a specific entity, promoting code organization and reusability.

18. How do loops contribute to code execution in programming?

a) By providing names to entities

b) By encapsulating code logic

c) By controlling program flow and enabling repeated execution of code

d) By grouping and organizing data

Answer: c) By controlling program flow and enabling repeated execution of code

Explanation: Loops, such as for and while loops, enable the repeated execution of a block of code, contributing to the control flow of a program.

19. What is the primary purpose of dictionaries in programming?

a) Enhancing code execution speed

b) Encapsulating code logic

c) Grouping and organizing data as key-value pairs

d) Controlling program flow

Answer: c) Grouping and organizing data as key-value pairs

Explanation: Dictionaries in programming store data as key-value pairs, providing an efficient way to group and organize related information.

20. How does proper error handling contribute to code robustness?

a) By enhancing code execution speed

b) By providing a way to group and organize data

c) By managing errors and preventing abrupt program termination

d) By controlling program flow

Answer: c) By managing errors and preventing abrupt program termination

Explanation: Proper error handling components prevent abrupt program termination and provide graceful handling of unexpected errors, contributing to code robustness.

21. What is the significance of sets in programming?

a) Enhancing code execution speed

b) Encapsulating code logic

c) Grouping and organizing unique elements without duplicates

d) Controlling program flow

Answer: c) Grouping and organizing unique elements without duplicates

Explanation: Sets in programming store unique elements without duplicates, providing an efficient way to manage collections of distinct values.

22. Why is it important to use proper indentation and formatting in programming?

a) Enhancing code execution speed

b) Encapsulating code logic

c) Improving code readability and conveying logical structure

d) Controlling program flow

Answer: c) Improving code readability and conveying logical structure

Explanation: Proper indentation and formatting improve code readability, making it easier to understand the logical structure of the code.

23. How do code comments contribute to effective collaboration in programming?

a) By enhancing code execution speed

b) By providing a way to group and organize data

c) By facilitating collaboration and improving code documentation

d) By controlling program flow

Answer: c) By facilitating collaboration and improving code documentation

Explanation: Code comments provide additional information, facilitating collaboration among developers and improving overall code documentation.

24. Why is modularization important in programming?

a) Enhancing code execution speed

b) Encapsulating code logic

c) Breaking down a program into smaller, independent modules for code reusability

d) Controlling program flow

Answer: c) Breaking down a program into smaller, independent modules for code reusability

Explanation: Modularization involves breaking down a program into smaller, independent modules or functions, promoting code reusability and maintainability.

25. How do naming conventions contribute to code consistency?

a) By enhancing code execution speed

b) By providing a way to group and organize data

c) By improving code documentation and ensuring consistent naming of entities

d) By controlling program flow

Answer: c) By improving code documentation and ensuring consistent naming of entities

Explanation: Naming conventions improve code consistency by ensuring that entities are named in a consistent and meaningful manner, enhancing code documentation.

26. In programming, what is the primary role of functions with parameters?

a) Enhancing code execution speed

b) Encapsulating code logic and promoting reusability

c) Providing names to entities in the code

d) Controlling program flow

Answer: b) Encapsulating code logic and promoting reusability

Explanation: Functions with parameters encapsulate code logic and promote reusability by allowing the function to operate on different input values.

27. How does inheritance contribute to code reuse in object-oriented programming?

a) By enhancing code execution speed

b) By providing a way to group and organize data

c) By allowing the creation of class hierarchies and promoting reuse of code logic

d) By controlling program flow

Answer: c) By allowing the creation of class hierarchies and promoting reuse of code logic

Explanation: Inheritance in object-oriented programming enables the creation of class hierarchies, promoting the reuse of code logic across related classes.

28. What is the role of loops in programming?

a) Enhancing code execution speed

b) Encapsulating code logic and promoting reusability

c) Controlling program flow and enabling repeated execution of code

d) Grouping and organizing data

Answer: c) Controlling program flow and enabling repeated execution of code

Explanation: Loops in programming control the flow of a program by enabling the repeated execution of a block of code. They are essential for iterating through data structures, performing repetitive tasks, and managing program flow.

29. How does encapsulation contribute to code security in programming?

a) By enhancing code execution speed

b) By providing a way to group and organize data

c) By hiding implementation details and preventing unintended access to data

d) By controlling program flow

Answer: c) By hiding implementation details and preventing unintended access to data

Explanation: Encapsulation hides implementation details, preventing unintended access to data and contributing to code security by controlling access to internal components.

30. What is the primary purpose of query languages in programming?

a) Enhancing code execution speed

b) Encapsulating code logic and promoting reusability

c) Grouping and organizing data for efficient database interactions

d) Controlling program flow

Answer: c) Grouping and organizing data for efficient database interactions

Explanation: Query languages, such as SQL (Structured Query Language), are used for grouping and organizing data in a database. They provide efficient mechanisms for interacting with databases by performing operations like data retrieval, insertion, updating, and deletion.

Chapter 5: Database Fundamentals

5.1 Explain Database Concepts and the Purpose of a Database

In the ever-expanding landscape of information technology, databases play a pivotal role in storing, organizing, and managing vast amounts of data. This section explores fundamental database concepts and delves into the purpose of a database, highlighting its usage, distinguishing between flat files and databases, and discussing key elements such as records and storage.

Usage of Database:

A database is a structured collection of data organized for efficient retrieval and manipulation. The primary purpose of a database is to provide a centralized and organized repository for storing and managing data. Unlike traditional methods of data storage, databases offer a systematic approach to handle large volumes of information, ensuring data integrity, security, and ease of access.

Key Points:

Data Integrity: Databases enforce rules and relationships, ensuring that data remains accurate and consistent.

Security: Access controls and authentication mechanisms safeguard sensitive information stored in databases.

Efficient Retrieval: Databases use indexing and querying mechanisms for swift data retrieval, enhancing performance.

Flat File vs. Database:

Understanding the distinction between flat files and databases is crucial. Flat files are unstructured data files that store information in a plain text format, lacking the relational structure and complexity of databases. On the other hand, databases provide a structured and organized environment with tables, relationships, and a querying language, facilitating efficient data management.

Key Points:

Flat Files: Simple, text-based storage without structured relationships.

Databases: Structured storage with tables, relationships, and a querying language (e.g., SQL).

Records:

A record is a fundamental unit of data in a database, representing a complete set of information about a single entity. Records are organized into tables, each containing rows and columns. Each column corresponds to a specific attribute, and each row represents a unique record.

Key Points:

Tables: Organized collections of records.

Attributes: Columns in a table represent specific attributes of the data.

Uniqueness: Each record is uniquely identified, often by a primary key.

Storage:

The storage aspect of databases involves the physical and logical organization of data. Databases use various storage mechanisms to ensure efficient data retrieval and management. This includes considerations such as indexing, partitioning, and data compression to optimize storage space and performance.

Key Points:

Indexing: Accelerates data retrieval by creating efficient access paths.

Partitioning: Distributes data across multiple storage devices for parallel processing.

Compression: Reduces storage space requirements by encoding data more efficiently.

A solid understanding of database fundamentals is essential for anyone venturing into the realm of information technology. Databases serve as the backbone for storing and managing data systematically, offering advantages in terms of data integrity, security, and efficient retrieval. Recognizing the distinctions between flat files and databases, comprehending the concept of records, and delving into storage mechanisms are crucial steps toward becoming proficient in database fundamentals. This knowledge forms the foundation for more advanced topics in database management and design.

5.2 Compare and Contrast Various Database Structures

The world of databases is diverse, accommodating various structures to suit different data storage and retrieval needs. This section delves into the comparison and contrast of structured, semi-structured, and non-structured databases, as well as the distinction between relational and non-relational databases.

Structured vs. Semi-Structured vs. Non-Structured Databases:

**1. Structured Databases:

Definition: Structured databases organize data in a well-defined and rigid schema. Data is stored in tables with predefined columns and data types.

Characteristics:

Schema: Clearly defined schema with fixed data types.

Examples: Relational databases like MySQL, Oracle, and PostgreSQL.

**2. Semi-Structured Databases:

Definition: Semi-structured databases do not require a predefined schema. They allow for flexibility in data representation and can accommodate varying data formats.

Characteristics:

Schema Flexibility: Can handle data with varying structures.

Examples: JSON, XML, and document-oriented databases.

**3. Non-Structured Databases:

Definition: Non-structured databases, often referred to as NoSQL databases, do not adhere to a fixed schema. They are designed to handle unstructured and unpredictable data.

Characteristics:

Schema-less: No predefined schema, allowing for dynamic and evolving data structures.

Examples: MongoDB, Cassandra, and CouchDB.

Relational Databases:

**1. Definition: Relational databases are structured databases that use a tabular format for storing and organizing data. They rely on the principles of relational algebra and have well-defined relationships between tables.

Characteristics:

Tables: Data is organized into tables with predefined relationships.

ACID Properties: Adhere to ACID (Atomicity, Consistency, Isolation, Durability) properties.

Examples: MySQL, PostgreSQL, Microsoft SQL Server.

Non-Relational Databases (NoSQL):

**2. Definition: Non-relational databases, or NoSQL databases, are designed to handle large volumes of unstructured and semi-structured data. They offer flexibility in terms of data representation and often prioritize horizontal scalability.

Characteristics:

Flexible Schema: Allow for dynamic and evolving data structures.

Scalability: Typically designed for horizontal scalability.

Examples: MongoDB, Cassandra, Redis.

Comparison and Contrast:

**1. Schema:

Structured: Has a rigid, predefined schema.

Semi-Structured: Allows flexibility in the schema.

Non-Structured (NoSQL): Typically schema-less or flexible schema.

**2. Data Relationships:

Structured: Relies on well-defined relationships between tables.

Semi-Structured: May represent relationships through nested structures or keys.

Non-Structured (NoSQL): Relationships can be handled through various mechanisms, such as embedding or referencing.

**3. Scalability:

Structured: Might face challenges in horizontal scalability.

Semi-Structured: Offers better scalability compared to traditional structured databases.

Non-Structured (NoSQL): Often designed for horizontal scalability, especially in distributed environments.

**4. Use Cases:

Structured: Suitable for applications with well-defined and stable data requirements.

Semi-Structured: Useful when data structures evolve or when dealing with diverse data formats.

Non-Structured (NoSQL): Ideal for handling unstructured or semi-structured data, high write loads, and horizontal scaling.

Understanding the distinctions between structured, semi-structured, and non-structured databases, as well as the differences between relational and non-relational databases, is crucial for choosing the right database model for specific use cases. Each type of database structure has its strengths and weaknesses, and the choice often depends on the nature of the data, scalability requirements, and the complexity of relationships within the data. As technology evolves, the database landscape continues to diversify, providing a range of options for efficiently managing and querying data.

5.3 Summarize Methods Used to Interface with Databases

Interfacing with databases is a critical aspect of database management, involving various methods and techniques to interact with and manipulate data. This section provides a summary of methods used to interface with databases, covering relational methods, database access methods, and export/import functionalities.

Relational Methods:

Relational databases adhere to the principles of relational algebra and utilize SQL (Structured Query Language) as the primary interface. SQL provides a standardized and powerful way to interact with relational databases. Key relational methods include:

SQL Queries: SQL queries are used to retrieve, manipulate, and manage data in relational databases. These queries can perform operations such as SELECT (retrieve data), INSERT (insert new data), UPDATE (modify existing data), and DELETE (remove data).

Stored Procedures: Relational databases support stored procedures, which are precompiled SQL statements stored in the database. They can be called by applications to perform complex operations on the database.

Triggers: Triggers are actions defined to occur automatically in response to specific events (e.g., data changes) in the database. They are useful for maintaining data integrity and enforcing business rules.

Database Access Methods:

Interfacing with databases requires effective access methods to retrieve, insert, update, and delete data. Key database access methods include:

ODBC (Open Database Connectivity): ODBC is a standard application programming interface (API) that enables applications to access various database systems using SQL. It provides a consistent interface, allowing applications to interact with different databases seamlessly.

JDBC (Java Database Connectivity): Similar to ODBC, JDBC is a Java-based API that facilitates database access for Java applications. It enables Java programs to interact with relational databases using SQL.

ORM (Object-Relational Mapping): ORM tools map object-oriented programming concepts to relational database concepts, providing a higher-level and more intuitive way to interact with databases. Popular ORM frameworks include Hibernate (for Java) and Entity Framework (for .NET).

Export/Import:

Exporting and importing data are essential functionalities for transferring data between databases or between a database and external systems. Key export/import methods include:

Data Dump (Export): A data dump involves exporting the entire database or specific tables in a format that can be easily imported into another system. Formats may include SQL scripts, CSV (Comma-Separated Values) files, or other structured formats.

Bulk Copy: Bulk copy methods allow the efficient transfer of large volumes of data between databases. This can involve specialized tools or database-specific commands to optimize data transfer.

ETL (Extract, Transform, Load): ETL processes are used to extract data from a source, transform it into the desired format, and load it into a target database. ETL tools automate and streamline this process.

Effectively interfacing with databases requires a comprehensive understanding of relational methods, database access methods, and export/import functionalities. Whether executing SQL queries, utilizing APIs like ODBC or JDBC, or transferring data through export/import processes, the chosen method depends on the specific needs of the application and the characteristics of the databases involved. As technology continues to evolve, new methods and tools are continually emerging to enhance the efficiency and versatility of database interaction.

Practice Question and Answers on Database Fundamentals

1. What is the primary purpose of a database?

a) Enhance code execution speed

b) Store, organize, and manage data systematically

c) Provide a way to group and organize data

d) Control program flow

Answer: b) Store, organize, and manage data systematically

Explanation: The primary purpose of a database is to provide a structured and organized repository for storing, managing, and retrieving data in a systematic manner.

2. How does a flat file differ from a database?

a) Flat files have a predefined schema, while databases do not.

b) Databases are text-based, while flat files use a tabular structure.

c) Flat files lack relationships, while databases use tables with predefined relationships.

d) Flat files are more scalable than databases.

Answer: c) Flat files lack relationships, while databases use tables with predefined relationships.

Explanation: Flat files are unstructured and lack the relational structure found in databases, where data is organized into tables with predefined relationships.

3. What is the purpose of records in a database?

a) Enhance code execution speed

b) Provide names to entities in the code

c) Represent a complete set of information about a single entity

d) Control program flow

Answer: c) Represent a complete set of information about a single entity

Explanation: Records in a database represent a complete set of information about a single entity and are organized into tables.

4. In a relational database, what is the purpose of a primary key?

a) Enhance code execution speed

b) Control program flow

c) Ensure data integrity by uniquely identifying each record in a table

d) Provide a way to group and organize data

Answer: c) Ensure data integrity by uniquely identifying each record in a table

Explanation: A primary key uniquely identifies each record in a table, ensuring data integrity and facilitating relationships between tables.

5. What distinguishes semi-structured databases from structured databases?

a) Semi-structured databases use SQL, while structured databases do not.

b) Semi-structured databases have a rigid schema, while structured databases allow flexibility.

c) Structured databases store data in a tabular format, while semi-structured databases allow varying data formats.

d) Semi-structured databases lack relationships between data.

Answer: c) Structured databases store data in a tabular format, while semi-structured databases allow varying data formats.

Explanation: Semi-structured databases allow for flexibility in data representation, supporting varying data formats, while structured databases use a tabular format.

6. What is a common API used for accessing various database systems?

a) JSON

b) ODBC (Open Database Connectivity)

c) XML

d) JDBC (Java Database Connectivity)

Answer: b) ODBC (Open Database Connectivity)

Explanation: ODBC is a standard API that allows applications to access various database systems using SQL.

7. What does ORM stand for in the context of databases?

a) Object-Relational Mapping

b) Organized Relationship Model

c) Object Retrieval Mechanism

d) Oriented Record Mapping

Answer: a) Object-Relational Mapping

Explanation: ORM stands for Object-Relational Mapping, a technique that maps object-oriented concepts to relational database concepts.

8. What is the purpose of triggers in a database?

a) Enhance code execution speed

b) Control program flow

c) Automatically perform actions in response to specific events

d) Provide a way to group and organize data

Answer: c) Automatically perform actions in response to specific events

Explanation: Triggers in a database are actions defined to occur automatically in response to specific events, such as data changes.

9. How does ETL contribute to data management?

a) Enhancing code execution speed

b) Facilitating data transfer between databases

c) Controlling program flow

d) Providing a way to group and organize data

Answer: b) Facilitating data transfer between databases

Explanation: ETL (Extract, Transform, Load) processes facilitate the extraction, transformation, and loading of data between databases.

10. What is the primary purpose of a data dump in database terminology?

a) Enhancing code execution speed

b) Backing up the entire database

c) Exporting data in a format for easy import into another system

d) Controlling program flow

Answer: c) Exporting data in a format for easy import into another system

Explanation: A data dump involves exporting data from a database in a format that can be easily imported into another system.

11. In a relational database, what is the purpose of the SELECT statement in SQL?

a) Inserting new data into the database

b) Retrieving data from one or more tables

c) Modifying existing data in the database

d) Deleting data from the database

Answer: b) Retrieving data from one or more tables

Explanation: The SELECT statement in SQL is used to retrieve data from one or more tables in a relational database.

12. What does ACID stand for in the context of relational databases?

a) Atomicity, Consistency, Isolation, Durability

b) Association, Cohesion, Isolation, Dependency

c) Access, Control, Isolation, Database

d) Atomic, Consecutive, Isolated, Durable

Answer: a) Atomicity, Consistency, Isolation, Durability

Explanation: ACID represents the key properties of a transaction in a relational database: Atomicity, Consistency, Isolation, and Durability.

13. What is the primary purpose of a foreign key in a relational database?

a) Enhance code execution speed

b) Control program flow

c) Establish a relationship between tables

d) Provide a way to group and organize data

Answer: c) Establish a relationship between tables

Explanation: A foreign key in a relational database establishes a relationship between tables by referencing the primary key of another table.

14. What is the role of indexing in database management?

a) Enhancing code execution speed

b) Facilitating data transfer between databases

c) Controlling program flow

d) Providing a way to group and organize data

Answer: a) Enhancing code execution speed

Explanation: Indexing in a database improves data retrieval speed by creating efficient access paths, reducing the need for full-table scans.

15. How does normalization contribute to database design?

a) Enhancing code execution speed

b) Facilitating data transfer between databases

c) Reducing data redundancy and improving data integrity

d) Providing a way to group and organize data

Answer: c) Reducing data redundancy and improving data integrity

Explanation: Normalization in database design involves organizing data to reduce data redundancy and improve data integrity.

16. What is the purpose of the GROUP BY clause in SQL?

a) Enhancing code execution speed

b) Grouping rows based on specified columns

c) Controlling program flow

d) Providing a way to group and organize data

Answer: b) Grouping rows based on specified columns

Explanation: The GROUP BY clause in SQL is used to group rows based on specified columns, often used in conjunction with aggregate functions.

17. How does the COMMIT statement affect database transactions?

a) Enhancing code execution speed

b) Finalizing and making permanent changes to a transaction

c) Controlling program flow

d) Providing a way to group and organize data

Answer: b) Finalizing and making permanent changes to a transaction

Explanation: The COMMIT statement in a database finalizes and makes permanent the changes made during a transaction.

18. What is the purpose of the CASCADE option in a foreign key constraint?

a) Enhancing code execution speed

b) Automatically updating or deleting related records when the referenced record changes

c) Controlling program flow

d) Providing a way to group and organize data

Answer: b) Automatically updating or deleting related records when the referenced record changes

Explanation: The CASCADE option in a foreign key constraint automatically updates or deletes related records when the referenced record changes.

19. How does a LEFT JOIN differ from an INNER JOIN in SQL?

a) Enhancing code execution speed

b) Controlling program flow

c) LEFT JOIN returns all records from the left table and matching records from the right table

d) INNER JOIN returns only matching records from both tables

Answer: c) LEFT JOIN returns all records from the left table and matching records from the right table

Explanation: In a LEFT JOIN, all records from the left table are returned, along with matching records from the right table. INNER JOIN returns only matching records from both tables.

20. What is the purpose of the HAVING clause in SQL?

a) Enhancing code execution speed

b) Filtering results based on aggregate functions

c) Controlling program flow

d) Providing a way to group and organize data

Answer: b) Filtering results based on aggregate functions

Explanation: The HAVING clause in SQL is used to filter the results of a query based on conditions applied to aggregate functions.

21. In database terminology, what is a stored procedure?

a) Enhancing code execution speed

b) A precompiled set of SQL statements stored in the database

c) Controlling program flow

d) Providing a way to group and organize data

Answer: b) A precompiled set of SQL statements stored in the database

Explanation: A stored procedure is a precompiled set of SQL statements stored in the database, which can be called by applications to perform specific operations.

22. What is the purpose of the ORDER BY clause in SQL?

a) Enhancing code execution speed

b) Sorting the result set based on specified columns

c) Controlling program flow

d) Providing a way to group and organize data

Answer: b) Sorting the result set based on specified columns

Explanation: The ORDER BY clause in SQL is used to sort the result set based on specified columns in ascending or descending order.

23. What does the term "Data Warehouse" refer to in the context of databases?

a) Enhancing code execution speed

b) A centralized repository for large volumes of historical and analytical data

c) Controlling program flow

d) Providing a way to group and organize data

Answer: b) A centralized repository for large volumes of historical and analytical data

Explanation: A Data Warehouse is a centralized repository for large volumes of historical and analytical data, often used for business intelligence and reporting.

24. What is the purpose of the ROLLBACK statement in database transactions?

a) Enhancing code execution speed

b) Undoing changes made during a transaction and restoring the data to its original state

c) Controlling program flow

d) Providing a way to group and organize data

Answer: b) Undoing changes made during a transaction and restoring the data to its original state

Explanation: The ROLLBACK statement in a database transaction is used to undo changes made during the transaction and restore the data to its original state.

25. How does the concept of database normalization contribute to efficient data storage?

a) Enhancing code execution speed

b) Reducing data redundancy and eliminating update anomalies

c) Controlling program flow

d) Providing a way to group and organize data

Answer: b) Reducing data redundancy and eliminating update anomalies

Explanation: Database normalization involves organizing data to reduce data redundancy and eliminate update anomalies, contributing to efficient data storage.

26. What is the purpose of the WHERE clause in SQL?

a) Enhancing code execution speed

b) Filtering results based on specified conditions

c) Controlling program flow

d) Providing a way to group and organize data

Answer: b) Filtering results based on specified conditions

Explanation: The WHERE clause in SQL is used to filter the results of a query based on specified conditions.

27. What is the significance of the COMMIT and ROLLBACK statements in transactions?

a) Enhancing code execution speed

b) Finalizing and making permanent changes (COMMIT) or undoing changes (ROLLBACK) made during a transaction

c) Controlling program flow

d) Providing a way to group and organize data

Answer: b) Finalizing and making permanent changes (COMMIT) or undoing changes (ROLLBACK) made during a transaction

Explanation: The COMMIT statement finalizes and makes permanent changes made during a transaction, while the ROLLBACK statement undoes those changes.

28. What is the primary purpose of the SQL UPDATE statement?

a) Enhancing code execution speed

b) Retrieving data from one or more tables

c) Modifying existing data in a table

d) Deleting data from a table

Answer: c) Modifying existing data in a table

Explanation: The SQL UPDATE statement is used to modify existing data in a table by changing values in specified columns.

29. How does the concept of a foreign key contribute to maintaining data integrity in a relational database?

a) Enhancing code execution speed

b) Automatically updating or deleting related records to maintain consistency

c) Controlling program flow

d) Providing a way to group and organize data

Answer: b) Automatically updating or deleting related records to maintain consistency

Explanation: A foreign key in a relational database automatically updates or deletes related records to maintain consistency and enforce referential integrity.

30. In SQL, what is the purpose of the JOIN operation in a query?

a) Enhancing code execution speed

b) Retrieving data from one or more tables

c) Modifying existing data in a table

d) Deleting data from a table

Answer: b) Retrieving data from one or more tables

Explanation: The JOIN operation in SQL is used to retrieve data from one or more tables by combining rows based on a related column between them.

Chapter 6 Security

6.1 Summarize Confidentiality, Integrity, and Availability Concerns

In the realm of information security, the fundamental principles of Confidentiality, Integrity, and Availability (CIA) form the bedrock for designing robust and secure systems. Let's delve into each concern:

Confidentiality Concerns:

Definition: Confidentiality ensures that sensitive information is accessible only to authorized individuals or systems.

Key Points:

Access Control: Implementing access controls such as authentication and authorization mechanisms ensures that only authorized users have access to confidential data.

Encryption: Employing encryption techniques protects data during transmission and storage, rendering it unreadable to unauthorized parties.

Data Classification: Classifying data based on sensitivity allows organizations to apply appropriate protection measures to safeguard information according to its importance.

Secure Communication Channels: Using secure communication channels, such as Virtual Private Networks (VPNs), ensures that data remains confidential during transit over networks.

Employee Training: Educating employees on the importance of confidentiality and security policies helps prevent inadvertent disclosures.

Integrity Concerns:

Definition: Integrity ensures that data remains accurate, unaltered, and reliable throughout its lifecycle.

Key Points:

Data Validation: Implementing input validation and verification mechanisms ensures that only valid and accurate data is processed and stored.

Checksums and Hashing: Employing checksums and cryptographic hashing techniques enables the detection of data tampering or corruption.

Version Control: Implementing version control mechanisms helps track changes to data, allowing for the identification of unauthorized modifications.

Access Logging: Maintaining detailed access logs allows organizations to trace and audit changes to data, promoting accountability.

Database Constraints: Applying integrity constraints within databases, such as primary keys and foreign keys, helps maintain data consistency and reliability.

Availability Concerns:

Definition: Availability ensures that systems and data are accessible and operational when needed.

Key Points:

Redundancy: Implementing redundancy, such as backup systems and failover mechanisms, ensures continuity in the event of hardware failures or other disruptions.

Distributed Systems: Utilizing distributed systems and load balancing helps distribute workloads, preventing bottlenecks and enhancing overall system availability.

Incident Response Planning: Developing incident response plans and disaster recovery strategies prepares organizations to mitigate the impact of disruptions promptly.

Network Security: Protecting against Distributed Denial of Service (DDoS) attacks and implementing firewalls safeguards network availability.

Regular Maintenance: Conducting regular maintenance, updates, and patches helps prevent system vulnerabilities and ensures ongoing availability.

Confidentiality, Integrity, and Availability are inseparable components of a comprehensive security strategy. By addressing these concerns, organizations can build resilient and secure systems that protect sensitive information, maintain data accuracy, and ensure uninterrupted access to critical resources. A holistic approach to security, encompassing policies, technologies, and user education, is essential for mitigating risks and fostering a secure computing environment.

6.2 Explain Methods to Secure Devices and Best Practices

In the modern digital landscape, securing devices such as mobile devices and workstations is paramount to safeguarding sensitive information and maintaining a secure computing environment. Let's explore effective methods and best practices for securing devices:

Securing Devices (Mobile/Workstation):

Device Encryption:

Method: Implement full-disk encryption to protect the entire storage on the device. This ensures that even if the device is lost or stolen, unauthorized users cannot access the data without the encryption key.

Best Practice: Enforce encryption for both mobile devices and workstations to protect sensitive data stored on them.

Authentication Mechanisms:

Method: Utilize strong authentication methods, such as biometrics (fingerprint, facial recognition) and multi-factor authentication (MFA), to enhance access control.

Best Practice: Require users to use strong and unique passwords along with an additional layer of authentication for increased security.

Regular Software Updates:

Method: Keep operating systems, applications, and security software up-to-date with the latest patches and updates.

Best Practice: Enable automatic updates to ensure that devices are protected against known vulnerabilities, reducing the risk of exploitation.

Mobile Device Management (MDM):

Method: Implement MDM solutions for mobile devices to enforce security policies, track devices, and remotely wipe data in case of loss or theft.

Best Practice: Configure MDM settings to enforce strong passcodes, encrypt data, and restrict the installation of unauthorized apps.

Firewalls and Antivirus Software:

Method: Activate firewalls on workstations and use reputable antivirus software to protect against malware and unauthorized network access.

Best Practice: Regularly update antivirus definitions and configure firewalls to allow only necessary network traffic.

Secure Wi-Fi Connections:

Method: Connect to secure and encrypted Wi-Fi networks. Avoid using public Wi-Fi for sensitive activities.

Best Practice: Use Virtual Private Networks (VPNs) to encrypt internet traffic, especially when accessing sensitive information over public networks.

Data Backups:

Method: Regularly back up important data to prevent loss in case of device failure, theft, or ransomware attacks.

Best Practice: Store backups in secure locations and periodically test the restoration process to ensure data recoverability.

Device Use Best Practices:

User Education:

Method: Conduct regular security awareness training to educate users about phishing attacks, social engineering, and other security threats.

Best Practice: Encourage users to report suspicious activities and adhere to security policies.

Remote Work Security:

Method: Implement secure remote work practices, including the use of Virtual Private Networks (VPNs) and secure communication tools.

Best Practice: Establish clear remote work policies and guidelines for securing devices outside the corporate network.

Access Controls:

Method: Implement the principle of least privilege, ensuring that users have the minimum level of access necessary to perform their job functions.

Best Practice: Regularly review and update access permissions based on job roles and responsibilities.

Physical Security:

Method: Secure physical access to devices by using locks, access cards, and surveillance.

Best Practice: Educate users on the importance of physically securing their devices and reporting lost or stolen devices promptly.

Application Whitelisting:

Method: Allow only approved and necessary applications to run on devices, preventing the execution of unauthorized or malicious software.

Best Practice: Regularly review and update the list of approved applications to align with business needs.

Incident Response Planning:

Method: Develop and regularly update an incident response plan to effectively respond to security incidents.

Best Practice: Conduct periodic drills to test the incident response plan and ensure a swift and coordinated response in case of a security incident.

By implementing these methods and best practices, organizations can significantly enhance the security posture of their devices, mitigating the risk of unauthorized access, data breaches, and other security threats. Regularly reassessing and adapting security measures in response to emerging threats is crucial for maintaining an effective security strategy.

6.3 Summarize Behavioral Security Concepts

In the realm of information security, understanding and promoting behavioral security concepts are crucial for establishing a culture of awareness, responsibility, and respect for privacy. Two key aspects to consider are expectations of privacy when using written policies and procedures, as well as the handling of confidential information.

Expectations of Privacy when Using Written Policies and Procedures:

Policy Acknowledgment:

Concept: Users should acknowledge and understand the organization's written security policies and procedures.

Importance: Acknowledgment indicates that individuals are aware of the established rules and guidelines for securing information.

User Training and Education:

Concept: Organizations should provide comprehensive training to users regarding the expectations of privacy outlined in written policies.

Importance: Education ensures that users are informed about the importance of privacy, security best practices, and potential consequences of policy violations.

Communication of Expectations:

Concept: Clearly communicate the expectations of privacy and security measures to all users within the organization.

Importance: Transparent communication fosters a culture of accountability, making users aware of their responsibilities in maintaining information security.

Regular Policy Reviews:

Concept: Periodically review and update written policies to align with evolving security threats and organizational needs.

Importance: Regular reviews help ensure that policies remain relevant and effective in addressing emerging challenges and technology changes.

Enforcement Mechanisms:

Concept: Establish clear consequences for policy violations, outlining disciplinary actions for non-compliance.

Importance: A well-defined enforcement framework encourages adherence to policies and discourages behavior that could compromise security.

Handling of Confidential Information:

Data Classification:

Concept: Clearly define and classify different types of information based on sensitivity.

Importance: Classification helps users identify confidential information and apply appropriate security measures based on the level of sensitivity.

Need-to-Know Principle:

Concept: Limit access to confidential information to individuals who have a legitimate need to know.

Importance: Adhering to the need-to-know principle minimizes the risk of unauthorized access and reduces the surface area for potential breaches.

Secure Storage and Transmission:

Concept: Employ secure storage methods and encryption when transmitting confidential information.

Importance: Secure storage and transmission safeguard sensitive data from unauthorized access, interception, or compromise.

Data Handling Procedures:

Concept: Establish and communicate clear procedures for handling, sharing, and disposing of confidential information.

Importance: Well-defined procedures ensure consistent and secure practices in the lifecycle management of confidential data.

User Accountability:

Concept: Foster a sense of accountability among users regarding the handling of confidential information.

Importance: Users who understand their accountability are more likely to exercise caution and diligence in their interactions with sensitive data.

Monitoring and Auditing:

Concept: Implement monitoring and auditing mechanisms to track access to and usage of confidential information.

Importance: Monitoring helps identify suspicious activities, detect potential breaches, and ensures compliance with security policies.

By emphasizing these behavioral security concepts, organizations can establish a security-conscious culture where individuals recognize the significance of privacy, actively contribute to maintaining confidentiality, and understand their role in upholding information security standards. Cultivating a security-aware mindset among users is a proactive approach to mitigating risks and building a resilient security posture.

6.4 Compare and Contrast Authentication, Authorization, Accounting, and Non-Repudiation Concepts

In the field of information security, several key concepts play crucial roles in safeguarding data and systems. Authentication, authorization, accounting, and non-repudiation are fundamental principles that collectively contribute to a robust security framework. Let's compare and contrast these concepts:

Authentication:

Definition: Authentication is the process of verifying the identity of a user, system, or entity attempting to access a resource or system.

Purpose:

Verify Identity: Ensures that the claimed identity is accurate.

Access Control: Grants access only to authenticated and authorized entities.

Methods:

Password-based: Users provide a secret password.

Biometric: Use of fingerprints, facial recognition, etc.

Token-based: Access granted with a physical or digital token.

Authorization:

Definition: Authorization determines the level of access and actions that an authenticated user, system, or entity is allowed to perform.

Purpose:

Access Control: Grants or denies permissions based on roles or privileges.

Resource Protection: Ensures sensitive data or functionalities are only accessible to authorized entities.

Implementation:

Role-Based Access Control (RBAC): Assigns permissions based on user roles.

Access Control Lists (ACLs): Specifies individual user permissions.

Accounting:

Definition: Accounting, also known as auditing or logging, involves tracking and recording activities and events within a system.

Purpose:

Monitoring and Analysis: Records actions for later analysis or investigation.

Compliance: Supports compliance requirements by maintaining an audit trail.

Components:

Audit Logs: Records events such as logins, file accesses, or configuration changes.

Monitoring Tools: Automated systems that alert on suspicious activities.

Non-Repudiation:

Definition: Non-repudiation ensures that a user or entity cannot deny the authenticity or origin of a message or action.

Purpose:

Legal Validity: Provides evidence in legal disputes by preventing parties from denying their actions.

Trust and Accountability: Enhances trust in digital transactions by ensuring accountability.

Techniques:

Digital Signatures: Cryptographically ensures the authenticity of a message.

Timestamps: Records the time of a transaction, preventing denial of involvement.

Comparison and Contrast:

Authentication vs. Authorization:

Authentication verifies identity, while authorization determines access rights.

Authentication ensures the right person or system is accessing resources, while authorization determines what actions that entity can perform.

Authorization vs. Accounting:

Authorization sets permissions based on roles or rules, while accounting records actions taken by authenticated entities.

Authorization defines the level of access, while accounting maintains a record of how that access is used.

Accounting vs. Non-Repudiation:

Accounting tracks and records system activities, while non-repudiation ensures the integrity and authenticity of those records.

Accounting provides a log of events, while non-repudiation prevents parties from denying their involvement in those events.

Non-Repudiation vs. Authentication:

Non-repudiation ensures that a party cannot deny their actions, while authentication verifies the identity of that party.

Non-repudiation adds a layer of trust to digital transactions, while authentication ensures that trust is established with the right entity.

In summary, these security concepts work in tandem to create a comprehensive and layered security posture. Authentication ensures that the right entities gain access, authorization determines what they can do, accounting logs their activities, and non-repudiation prevents denial of involvement. Together, these concepts form a robust framework for securing digital systems and transactions.

6.5 Explain Password Best Practices

Passwords are a critical component of user authentication and play a key role in securing digital accounts and systems. Implementing strong password practices is essential to mitigate the risk of unauthorized access. Here are key best practices for managing passwords:

1. Password Length:

Best Practice: Encourage the use of long passwords.

Explanation: Longer passwords provide increased security as they offer a larger combination of characters, making them more resistant to brute-force attacks. A minimum length of 12 characters is generally recommended.

2. Password Complexity:

Best Practice: Promote the use of complex passwords.

Explanation: Complex passwords include a combination of uppercase and lowercase letters, numbers, and special characters. This complexity enhances the password's strength, making it more challenging for attackers to guess or crack.

3. Password History:

Best Practice: Implement a password history policy.

Explanation: Prevent users from reusing a certain number of previous passwords. This measure ensures that individuals do not cyclically revert to previously used passwords, enhancing security.

4. Password Expiration:

Best Practice: Enforce periodic password changes.

Explanation: Set a policy that requires users to change their passwords regularly. This reduces the risk of compromised passwords persisting over an extended period, especially in the event of a security incident.

5. Password Reuse Across Sites:

Best Practice: Discourage the use of identical passwords across multiple sites.

Explanation: Using unique passwords for different accounts prevents a security breach on one platform from compromising other accounts.

6. Password Managers:

Best Practice: Encourage the use of password management tools.

Explanation: Password managers help users generate, store, and manage complex passwords for various accounts securely. They alleviate the burden of remembering multiple passwords and contribute to better overall password hygiene.

7. Password Reset Process:

Best Practice: Implement a secure password reset process.

Explanation: Ensure that password reset mechanisms are secure and require multi-factor authentication. This prevents unauthorized individuals from gaining access through compromised or reset passwords.

8. Multi-Factor Authentication (MFA):

Best Practice: Enable multi-factor authentication.

Explanation: MFA adds an extra layer of security by requiring users to provide multiple forms of identification before granting access. This significantly enhances the overall security of accounts.

9. User Education:

Best Practice: Educate users on password security best practices.

Explanation: Regularly provide training and awareness programs to users, emphasizing the importance of strong passwords, secure practices, and the risks associated with weak or compromised passwords.

10. Account Lockout Policies:

Best Practice: Implement account lockout policies.

Explanation: Set policies that automatically lock user accounts after a certain number of failed login attempts. This helps protect against brute-force attacks.

By incorporating these password best practices into organizational policies and user education programs, entities can significantly enhance the security of their systems and mitigate the risks associated with compromised passwords.

6.6 Explain Common Uses of Encryption

Encryption is a fundamental technique in information security that involves converting data into a secure and unreadable format to protect it from unauthorized access. Common uses of encryption include securing communication, protecting data at rest, and ensuring the confidentiality of sensitive information.

Plain Text vs. Cipher Text:

Explanation:

Plain Text: Refers to the original, human-readable form of data.

Cipher Text: Represents the encrypted form of data, which is not easily readable without the decryption key.

Common Uses:

Secure Communication: Encryption is applied to messages or data before transmission, transforming plain text into cipher text. This ensures that even if intercepted, the content remains confidential.

Data at Rest:

Explanation:

Data at Rest: Refers to stored data, whether on physical devices like hard drives or in the cloud.

Encryption at Rest: Involves encrypting data when it is not actively being used.

Common Uses:

File and Disk Encryption: Encrypting files, folders, or entire disk drives protects data stored on devices from unauthorized access, especially in the event of theft or loss.

Database Encryption: Encrypting data within databases adds an extra layer of security, ensuring that even if the database is compromised, the data remains unreadable without the appropriate decryption key.

Data in Transit:

Explanation:

Data in Transit: Describes data moving between devices or across networks.

Encryption in Transit: Involves securing data as it travels from one point to another.

Common Uses:

Secure Sockets Layer (SSL) and Transport Layer Security (TLS): Used to encrypt data exchanged between web servers and browsers during online transactions, protecting sensitive information such as login credentials and credit card details.

Virtual Private Network (VPN): Encrypts data transmitted between a user and a remote server, ensuring privacy and security, especially when accessing networks over the internet.

Additional Common Uses:

Email Encryption:

Explanation: Encrypting email content and attachments to prevent unauthorized access during transmission.

Common Use: Protecting sensitive information shared via email.

Endpoint Encryption:

Explanation: Encrypting data on individual devices (endpoints) such as laptops, smartphones, or tablets.

Common Use: Safeguarding data stored on devices, particularly in the event of loss or theft.

Voice over Internet Protocol (VoIP) Encryption:

Explanation: Securing voice communication over the internet by encrypting audio data.

Common Use: Ensuring the confidentiality of voice conversations conducted through internet-based communication platforms.

Cloud Storage Encryption:

Explanation: Encrypting data stored in cloud-based storage services.

Common Use: Protecting files and information stored in cloud repositories against unauthorized access.

Encryption serves as a critical tool in maintaining the confidentiality and integrity of data, whether it is in transit across networks, at rest on storage devices, or being communicated between users. Implementing encryption practices is essential for organizations and individuals looking to secure sensitive information in today's digital landscape.

6.7 Explain Business Continuity Concepts

Business continuity involves planning and implementing strategies to ensure that essential business functions can continue during and after disruptions, emergencies, or disasters. Two key concepts in business continuity are fault tolerance and disaster recovery.

Fault Tolerance:

Explanation:

Fault Tolerance: Refers to a system's ability to continue operating with minimal disruption in the event of a component failure or fault.

Key Characteristics:

Redundancy: Incorporating duplicate components or systems to provide backup in case of a failure.

Automated Failover: Automated processes that redirect operations to redundant components when a fault is detected.

Common Uses:

High-Availability Systems: Systems that demand constant uptime, such as critical infrastructure or financial services, often implement fault-tolerant architectures to minimize downtime.

Benefits:

Continuous Operations: Ensures that critical functions remain operational, reducing the impact of component failures.

Disaster Recovery:

Explanation:

Disaster Recovery (DR): Involves planning and implementing strategies for the recovery of IT systems, data, and business operations in the aftermath of a disaster or significant disruption.

Key Components:

Backup and Restoration: Regularly backing up data and systems to enable swift recovery in the event of data loss or system failure.

Alternate Sites: Establishing alternate physical or virtual locations to resume operations if primary facilities are unavailable.

Common Practices:

Data Replication: Replicating data in real-time to a secondary location to ensure the availability of up-to-date information.

Testing and Drills: Conducting regular testing and drills to verify the effectiveness of disaster recovery plans and train personnel.

Benefits:

Minimized Downtime: Enables organizations to recover quickly from disasters, minimizing the impact on business operations.

Data Integrity: Ensures the integrity and availability of critical data, preventing permanent loss.

Integration of Fault Tolerance and Disaster Recovery:

Synergy:

Combined Approach: Organizations often integrate fault tolerance and disaster recovery to create a comprehensive business continuity strategy.

Continuous Improvement: Regular assessments and updates to these strategies ensure they remain effective in the face of evolving risks and technology changes.

Business continuity, encompassing fault tolerance and disaster recovery, is essential for organizations to withstand and recover from disruptions. Whether dealing with hardware failures, cyberattacks, or natural disasters, a well-designed and regularly tested business continuity plan ensures that critical business functions can persist, minimizing the impact on operations and maintaining the trust of stakeholders.

Practice Questions and Answers on Security

1. Question: What is the primary purpose of authentication in information security?

a) Ensuring data integrity

b) Protecting against malware

c) Verifying the identity of users or systems

d) Monitoring network traffic

Answer: c) Verifying the identity of users or systems

2. Question: What does SSL stand for in the context of internet security?

a) Secure Socket Layer

b) Super Speedy Login

c) Simple System Language

d) Standard Security Layer

Answer: a) Secure Socket Layer

3. Question: In the CIA triad, which component focuses on ensuring that information is available when needed?

a) Confidentiality

b) Integrity

c) Availability

d) Authorization

Answer: c) Availability

4. Question: What is the purpose of a firewall in network security?

a) Encrypting data

b) Blocking unauthorized access

c) Monitoring user activity

d) Managing network traffic

Answer: b) Blocking unauthorized access

5. Question: What is the primary goal of encryption in information security?

a) Ensuring data availability

b) Protecting against malware

c) Preventing unauthorized access

d) Monitoring network traffic

Answer: c) Preventing unauthorized access

6. Question: What is the term for the practice of tricking individuals into divulging sensitive information by pretending to be a trustworthy entity?

a) Spoofing

b) Phishing

c) Hacking

d) Denial of Service

Answer: b) Phishing

7. Question: Which authentication method involves using something a user knows, such as a password?

a) Biometric authentication

b) Two-factor authentication

c) Single sign-on

d) Knowledge-based authentication

Answer: d) Knowledge-based authentication

8. Question: What does the acronym VPN stand for in the context of network security?

a) Virtual Private Network

b) Very Private Connection

c) Verified Protection Network

d) Virtual Personal Node

Answer: a) Virtual Private Network

9. Question: What is the primary purpose of a Virtual Private Network (VPN)?

a) Encrypting data in transit

b) Blocking malicious websites

c) Managing network traffic

d) Securing physical access to servers

Answer: a) Encrypting data in transit

10. Question: What is the primary purpose of a biometric authentication system?

a) Protecting against malware

b) Encrypting data

c) Verifying identity using physical or behavioral characteristics

d) Monitoring network traffic

Answer: c) Verifying identity using physical or behavioral characteristics

11. Question: In the context of data security, what does the term "Data at Rest" refer to?

a) Data being transmitted over a network

b) Data stored on physical or virtual devices

c) Data actively being used by applications

d) Data subject to encryption

Answer: b) Data stored on physical or virtual devices

12. Question: What is the primary purpose of penetration testing in cybersecurity?

a) Developing software

b) Identifying vulnerabilities in systems

c) Monitoring network traffic

d) Encrypting data

Answer: b) Identifying vulnerabilities in systems

13. Question: Which of the following is an example of a physical security measure?

a) Firewalls

b) Encryption

c) Biometric access controls

d) Security policies

Answer: c) Biometric access controls

14. Question: What does the term "Social Engineering" refer to in the context of security?

a) Implementing firewalls

b) Manipulating individuals to divulge sensitive information

c) Encrypting data

d) Monitoring network traffic

Answer: b) Manipulating individuals to divulge sensitive information

15. Question: What is the primary purpose of role-based access control (RBAC)?

a) Encrypting data

b) Managing network traffic

c) Granting permissions based on user roles

d) Blocking unauthorized access

Answer: c) Granting permissions based on user roles

16. Question: What is the purpose of a security audit in information security?

a) Encrypting data

b) Identifying security vulnerabilities and ensuring compliance

c) Blocking unauthorized access

d) Monitoring network traffic

Answer: b) Identifying security vulnerabilities and ensuring compliance

17. Question: What is the primary goal of incident response in cybersecurity?

a) Encrypting data

b) Identifying security vulnerabilities

c) Responding to and mitigating security incidents

d) Blocking unauthorized access

Answer: c) Responding to and mitigating security incidents

18. Question: What does the term "Phishing" refer to in the context of cybersecurity?

a) Encrypting data

b) Manipulating individuals to divulge sensitive information

c) Blocking unauthorized access

d) Monitoring network traffic

Answer: b) Manipulating individuals to divulge sensitive information

19. Question: What is the primary purpose of a security policy in an organization?

a) Managing network traffic

b) Encrypting data

c) Providing guidelines for secure behavior and practices

d) Blocking unauthorized access

Answer: c) Providing guidelines for secure behavior and practices

20. Question: What is the purpose of a security token in two-factor authentication?

a) Encrypting data

b) Blocking unauthorized access

c) Providing an additional layer of authentication

d) Managing network traffic

Answer: c) Providing an additional layer of authentication

21. Question: What does the term "Zero-Day Exploit" refer to in cybersecurity?

a) A software vulnerability known to attackers for zero days

b) An attack that occurs on the first day of a security breach

c) A previously unknown software vulnerability exploited by attackers

d) A strategy to protect against malware

Answer: c) A previously unknown software vulnerability exploited by attackers

22. Question: What is the purpose of a security awareness training program?

a) Blocking unauthorized access

b) Identifying security vulnerabilities

c) Educating individuals on security risks and best practices

d) Monitoring network traffic

Answer: c) Educating individuals on security risks and best practices

23. Question: What does the term "BYOD" stand for in the context of security?

a) Bring Your Own Device

b) Backup Your Operating System Daily

c) Block Your Online Data

d) Biometric Yield On Demand

Answer: a) Bring Your Own Device

24. Question: What is the primary goal of Multi-Factor Authentication (MFA)?

a) Encrypting data

b) Blocking unauthorized access

c) Providing multiple layers of authentication

d) Managing network traffic

Answer: c) Providing multiple layers of authentication

25. Question: What is the purpose of a security incident response plan?

a) Identifying security vulnerabilities

b) Blocking unauthorized access

c) Responding to and mitigating security incidents

d) Encrypting data

Answer: c) Responding to and mitigating security incidents

26. Question: What is the primary purpose of a security patch in cybersecurity?

a) Identifying security vulnerabilities

b) Blocking unauthorized access

c) Updating and fixing security flaws in software

d) Monitoring network traffic

Answer: c) Updating and fixing security flaws in software

27. Question: What does the term "Man-in-the-Middle Attack" refer to in cybersecurity?

a) A physical intrusion into a secure facility

b) A network attack that involves intercepting communication between two parties

c) A type of malware that steals sensitive information

d) A strategy to block unauthorized access

Answer: b) A network attack that involves intercepting communication between two parties

28. Question: What is the purpose of a security risk assessment in an organization?

a) Identifying security vulnerabilities

b) Blocking unauthorized access

c) Assessing and mitigating potential security risks

d) Monitoring network traffic

Answer: c) Assessing and mitigating potential security risks

29. Question: What does the term "Ransomware" refer to in cybersecurity?

a) A type of malware that steals sensitive information

b) A strategy to block unauthorized access

c) Malicious software that encrypts files and demands payment for their release

d) A physical intrusion into a secure facility

Answer: c) Malicious software that encrypts files and demands payment for their release

30. Question: What is the primary purpose of a security perimeter in network security?

a) Encrypting data

b) Blocking unauthorized access

c) Managing network traffic

d) Identifying security vulnerabilities

Answer: b) Blocking unauthorized access

Questions and Answers

Questions

Question 1:

While browsing the Internet, a threatening message suddenly appears on Margot's screen demanding a payment. If she doesn't pay, the software will disable her system. What type of malware infection hit Margot's computer?

1. Spyware

2. Virus

3. Ransomware

4. Adware

Question 2:

Your web browser performance has suffered after a few weeks of installing new free software. What should you do to improve web browser performance?

1. Remove proxy server settings

2. Remove script-blocking settings

3. Remove the malware scanner

4. Remove browser add-ons

Question 3:

You are configuring a specialized 32-bit hardware device used for aviation mechanical testing. The device RAM can be upgraded to the maximum allowed with 32-bit computing. You need to add memory to the device. What is the maximum amount of memory the device can accommodate?

1. 8 GB

2. 4 GB

3. 16 GB

4. 32 Gb

Question 4:

Which of the following addresses is expressed in binary format?

1.   192.168.1.1

2.   2001:0db8:85a3:0000:0000:8a2e:0370:7334

3.   11111111.00000000.00000000.00000000

4.   www.google.com

Question 5:

You have configured an in-memory database cache to improve database query performance. What type of storage is this?

1.   Hard disk storage

2.   Solid-state drive storage

3.   RAM storage

4.   Optical storage

Question 6:

Which of the following terms is most closely related to measuring database disk performance?

1.   Latency

2.   Bandwidth

3.   Throughput

4.   Disk space

Question 7:

Your software development team recommends building a new custom software application as an n-tiered application. Which of the following are benefits that will be realized from this design strategy? (Choose three.)

1.   Improved performance

2.   Increased scalability

3.   Enhanced security

4.   Hard maintenance

Question 8:

Of the following technologies, which provides the highest throughput and the lowest latency?

1.   Ethernet

2.   Wi-Fi

3.   Cellular data

4.   Infrared

Question 9:

Art wants to make a backup of some files. Which optical technology offers the most capacity?

1.   CD-ROM

2.   DVD-ROM

3.   Blu-Ray Disc

4.   HD-DVD

Question 10:

Erin got a gift of a new inkjet printer, and she wants to make sure her computer has a compatible port to plug it in. When she looks at the back of her printer, she sees a lot of port types. Which ones will most likely work for her printer? (Choose two.)

1.   USB Type-C

2.   Parallel Port

3.   Ethernet Port

4.   USB Type-A

5.   Bluetooth

Question 11:

Pablo receives an email message formatted to appear as if his bank sent it. The email message explains that Pablo must confirm the name, address, and Social Security number listed on the bank account. Which of the following best describes the security threat?

1.   Spoofing

2.   Virus

3.   Adware

4.   Phishing

Question 12:

You are configuring a second disk in your Linux computer, and the file system on the disk must support journaling. Which file system should you use?

1.   FAT32

2.   NTFS

3.   Ext4

4.   XFS

Question 13:

When Rob returns from a conference in Vegas, his anti-malware software detects a virus on the thumb drive he used at the conference. He knows for certain that he used the thumb drive in one of the public kiosks to transfer files. What is the most likely cause of the infection?

1.   Social Engineering

2.   Drive-by downloads

3.   Rogue software

4.   Phishing Scams

Question 14:

You are adding metadata to product documentation files on a file server for your company's soon to be released product. The metadata will be used for long-term data classification and archiving purposes. Which of the following is the best category for this type of file?

1.   Confidential files

2.   Marketing collateral

3.   Engineering specifications

4.   Archived data

Question 15:

Which device will respond most quickly to disk read and writes?

1.   Hard Disk Drive (HDD)

2.   Solid State Drive (SSD)

3.   Hybrid Drive (HDD/SSD)

4.   Optical Disk Drive (ODD)

Question 16:

Cindy needs to describe ransomware to her boss. What explanation should she use?

1.   Ransomware is a type of malicious software that infects a computer system and restricts access to its files and data, typically by encrypting them. The attacker then demands payment in exchange for a decryption key to restore access to the affected data.

2.   Ransomware is a type of spyware that tracks the user's online activity and reports it back to the attacker.

3.   Ransomware is a type of malware that deletes the user's files and data permanently.

4.   Ransomware is a type of adware that displays unwanted advertisements and pop-ups on the user's computer.

Question 17:

Which term best describes cloud software that does not need to be installed but instead runs within a web browser?

1.   SECaaS (Security as a Service)

2.   IaaS (Infrastructure as a Service)

3.   SaaS (Software as a Service)

4.   PaaS (Platform as a Service)

Question 18:

Judy browsed to a most trusted news site and unexpectedly got a bunch of pop-up ads. Worse, the site was really slow. What is the most likely problem?

1.   The workstation has been infected with malware

2.   The website has been infected with malware

3.   The workstation DNS cache is corrupted

4.   The web site certificate has expired

Question 19:

An employee, Severus, forgot his laptop at the airport. Severus is worried about unauthorized access. What could protect against data theft?

1.   Cable lock

2.   Requiring a username and password to access the laptop

3.   Installing anti-virus software

4.   Patching the OS and third-party software

5.   Fully Encrypting the hard drive

6.   Keeping sensitive information on a separate device

Question 20:

Sarah takes a tech call from a frantic user who claims that the printer won't print. At Sarah's suggestion that the printer requires special paper, the user takes a moment to switch the paper and can now print. What printer technology must this be?

1.   Dot Matrix Printer

2.   Laser Printer

3.   Thermal Printer

4.   Inkjet Printer

Question 21:

Your news web site allows user comments, links, and embedded files of various types. Developers in your company are creating a solution that will process and store these vast amounts of data. Which data solution should you use to store these vast amounts of data?

1.   Relational database management system (RDBMS)

2.   Column-oriented database management system

3.   Key-value store database management system

4.   Document-oriented database management system

Question 22:

You are planning the storage of customer data in a relational database. Among other items, the existing table has a field named "Customer Name" that contains both the first and last name. Because of the large amount of customer records, you need to ensure searching is as quick as possible. What should you do? (Choose two.)

1.   Break the data down into smaller fields

2.   Break the data down into smaller rows

3.   Break the data down into smaller records

4.   Break the data down into smaller columns

Question 23:

You are creating a custom application that will process orders from a web site. Your code needs a variable that will store mobile phone numbers for customers. What data type should you use for this variable?

1.   Integer

2.   Float

3.   String

4.   Boolean

Question 24:

Pranks R Us is a retail chain that sells prank items. You are planning a relational database design that will store retail inventory. Which data type should you choose for the Items In Stock column?

1. Boolean

2. Integer

3. Float

4. String

Question 25:

A fax machine requires a specific component to use POTS to send a fax. Select the best choice from this list.

1. Modem

2. Toner cartridge

3. Phone cord

4. Fax machine paper

Question 26:

Aria has a new SOHO router. What management configuration should she do first?

1. Disable the SSID

2. Disable Wi-Fi

3. Change the administrator password

4. Change the SSID

Question 27:

During which SDLC phase are software security fixes created and made available to consumers?

1. Implementation phase

2. Requirements Analysis phase

3. Design phase

4. Maintenance phase

5. Planning Phase

Question 28:

John purchased a new Apple iPad mobile device. Of the following, which should he do first when configuring Wi-Fi settings?

1.   John should first configure the screen lock.

2.   John should first configure his email.

3.   John should first turn on Wi-Fi on the device

4.   John should first locate Wi-Fi networks.

Question 29:

John is flying from Houston to Fresno to deliver top-secret plans from his company, Bayland Widgets. The plans are on his Android-based smartphone. What should he disable to make his phone secure from hackers? (Choose two.)

1.   Location Services

2.   Bluetooth

3.   Mobile Data

4.   Wi-Fi

5.   GPS

Question 30:

Which of the following items are related to the planning and design of a software solution?

1.   Testing and debugging

2.   Requirements gathering and analysis

3.   Implementation and deployment

4.   Maintenance and support

Answers and Explanations

Question 1:

Answer: C.

Margot's computer was infected with Ransomware.

Ransomware is a type of malicious software that encrypts a user's files, making them inaccessible. The attacker then demands a ransom payment in exchange for the decryption key, which is necessary to regain access to the encrypted files. In Margot's case, the threatening message that appeared on her screen demanding payment is an example of a ransomware attack.

Spyware is a type of malicious software that is designed to collect and transmit information about a user's activities without their knowledge or consent. It can also interfere with the normal functioning of a computer system.

A virus is a type of malware that infects a computer system by spreading from one file to another, replicating itself and potentially causing damage to the system.

Adware is a type of malicious software that displays unwanted advertisements on a user's computer, usually in the form of pop-up ads or banners. It can slow down the computer system and interfere with its normal functioning.

Question 2:

Answer: D.

Remove browser add-ons. Some browser extensions may consume excessive resources and slow down your browsing experience. Disabling or removing the extensions that you don't need can help improve performance.

Clear your browser cache and history: Over time, your browser cache can become cluttered, and the history can accumulate a lot of data. Clearing these can free up space and improve performance.

Update your browser to the latest version: Outdated browsers can have security vulnerabilities and performance issues. Updating to the latest version can improve performance and security.

Uninstalling the new free software: In some cases, the new software may be the cause of the slow performance. Uninstalling it can help to determine if this is the case and improve performance. However, it is important to exercise caution when uninstalling software as it may have dependencies and removing it could cause other problems.

Question 3:

Answer: A.

32-bit computing has a limit on the amount of RAM it can support. The maximum amount of RAM that can be addressed by a 32-bit operating system is 4 GB, with some operating systems being limited to only 3 GB. However, due to limitations of the system architecture and the memory addressing mechanism, the actual amount of usable memory is typically limited to around 3.2 GB to 3.5 GB.

In the case of the specialized hardware device, it may be limited to a lower amount of memory than the maximum theoretical limit for 32-bit computing, such as 8 GB. This could be due to hardware or firmware constraints, or simply to optimize the device's performance and stability. It's important to check the specifications for the device to determine the exact maximum amount of memory it can accommodate.

Question 4:

Answer: C.

• 192.168.1.1 is an IP address expressed in dotted decimal notation, which is a common way of representing IP addresses in human-readable form.

• 2001:0db8:85a3:0000:0000:8a2e:0370:7334 is an IPv6 address, expressed in colon-hexadecimal notation.

• 11111111.00000000.00000000.00000000 is a binary representation of an IP address. In binary format, each number in the address is represented as a 8-bit value, and the values are separated by a period.

• www.google.com is a domain name, not an IP address. IP addresses are expressed in binary, dotted decimal, or colon-hexadecimal notation, whereas domain names are expressed in human-readable text format.

Question 5:

Answer: C.

An in-memory database cache is stored in random-access memory (RAM), which is a type of volatile memory. RAM is fast, but its contents are lost when power is removed from the device. The purpose of the in-memory cache is to improve database query performance by storing frequently used data in RAM so that it can be quickly retrieved, rather than having to be retrieved from the slower hard disk or solid-state drive storage.

• Hard disk storage: A hard disk is a type of non-volatile storage that uses magnetic disks to store data. It is typically slower than RAM storage.

• Solid-state drive storage: A solid-state drive (SSD) is a type of non-volatile storage that uses flash memory to store data. It is faster than a hard disk, but still slower than RAM.

• RAM storage: RAM is a type of volatile memory that is used to store data temporarily. It is faster than hard disk and solid-state drive storage, but its contents are lost when power is removed from the device.

• Optical storage: Optical storage uses laser technology to read and write data to and from a disk. Examples of optical storage include CD, DVD, and Blu-ray discs. Optical storage is typically slower than RAM, hard disk, and solid-state drive storage.

Question 6:

Answer: A.

Latency is the time it takes for a disk operation to complete, such as reading or writing a block of data. It is a measure of the responsiveness of the disk, and it is a critical factor in database disk performance. Latency directly impacts the amount of time it takes to retrieve data from the disk, which in turn affects the overall performance of the database.

• Latency: The time it takes for a disk operation to complete, such as reading or writing a block of data.

• Bandwidth: The amount of data that can be transmitted in a given period of time, typically measured in bits per second.

• Throughput: The amount of data that can be processed in a given period of time, typically measured in operations per second or requests per second.

• Disk space: The amount of storage space available on a disk, typically measured in gigabytes (GB) or terabytes (TB). Disk space is not directly related to database disk performance, but it can affect performance if the disk becomes full and is unable to store new data.

Question 7:

Answer: A, B, C.

An n-tiered application is a type of software architecture that separates the application into multiple logical tiers, or layers. Each tier performs a specific set of functions and communicates with the other tiers to deliver the overall functionality of the application. This design strategy has several benefits:

• Improved performance: By separating the application into multiple tiers, each tier can be optimized for a specific set of functions, which can lead to improved performance.

For example, the presentation tier can be optimized for user interface (UI) performance, while the data tier can be optimized for data retrieval and storage performance.

• Increased scalability: N-tiered applications are designed to be scalable, meaning that they can be easily modified to accommodate changes in user or system requirements. For example, if the application needs to support more users, additional servers can be added to the application tier to handle the increased load.

• Enhanced security: By separating the application into multiple tiers, it becomes easier to secure each tier individually, as well as the communication between tiers. This can lead to a more secure overall application, as threats and vulnerabilities can be isolated and addressed at the appropriate tier.

• Simplified maintenance: N-tiered applications are designed to be modular, meaning that each tier can be maintained and updated independently. This can lead to simplified maintenance and a more efficient development process, as changes to one tier do not necessarily impact other tiers.

Question 8:

Answer: A.

Ethernet provides the highest throughput and the lowest latency of the technologies listed. Ethernet is a wired technology that uses physical cables to transmit data. It provides high-speed, reliable data transfer and is commonly used for local area networks (LANs) and wide area networks (WANs).

• Ethernet: Ethernet provides the highest throughput and the lowest latency of the technologies listed. It supports data transfer rates up to 10 Gbps and has low latency, making it suitable for high-speed data transfer and real-time applications.

• Wi-Fi: Wi-Fi is a wireless technology that uses radio waves to transmit data. While it provides high data transfer rates and low latency compared to cellular data, it is not as fast or reliable as Ethernet.

• Cellular data: Cellular data is a wireless technology that uses cellular networks to transmit data. While it provides high data transfer rates compared to infrared, it has higher latency and is less reliable than Ethernet and Wi-Fi.

• Infrared: Infrared is a wireless technology that uses infrared light to transmit data. While it provides a low-cost solution for short-range data transfer, it has the lowest data transfer rates and the highest latency of the technologies listed.

Question 9:

Answer: C.

Blu-Ray Disc is the optical technology that offers the most capacity. Blu-Ray Discs have the ability to store large amounts of data, with capacities ranging from 25 GB to 100 GB. This makes them ideal for backing up large amounts of data, such as high-definition video and other multimedia content.

• CD-ROM: CD-ROM (Compact Disc Read-Only Memory) has a capacity of 700 MB and is an older technology that is now largely replaced by other options.

• DVD-ROM: DVD-ROM (Digital Versatile Disc Read-Only Memory) has a capacity of 4.7 GB and is still used for backing up smaller amounts of data.

• Blu-Ray Disc: Blu-Ray Disc is the current optical technology offering the most capacity, with capacities ranging from 25 GB to 100 GB.

• HD-DVD: HD-DVD (High-Definition Digital Versatile Disc) was a competitor to the Blu-Ray format, but it lost the format war and is no longer used.

Question 10:

Answer: A, D.

Inkjet printers typically connect to a computer through a USB port. Both USB Type-C and USB Type-A are standard USB ports that are commonly found on modern computers.

• USB Type-C: USB Type-C is a newer type of USB port that is becoming increasingly common on modern computers and is fully compatible with most printers.

• Parallel Port: The parallel port is an older type of port that is not commonly found on modern computers and is typically not used to connect printers.

• Ethernet Port: An Ethernet port is used to connect devices to a network, not to connect printers directly to a computer.

• USB Type-A: USB Type-A is a standard USB port that is widely used to connect printers, as well as other devices, to computers.

Question 11:

Answer: D.

Phishing is a type of online scam where the attacker pretends to be a trustworthy entity, such as a bank, to trick the victim into revealing sensitive information, such as login credentials or personal information. In this case, the email message that Pablo received is a classic example of phishing.

- Phishing: Phishing is a form of social engineering that uses email, phone, or text messages to trick individuals into giving sensitive information, such as usernames, passwords, and credit card numbers, to an attacker.

- Spoofing: Spoofing is a type of cyber attack where an attacker falsifies information in the header of an email, text message, or other electronic communication, to make it appear as if it came from a different source.

- Virus: A virus is a type of malicious software that infects a computer, usually through an email attachment or malicious website, and can cause damage to the computer or steal sensitive information.

- Adware: Adware is a type of software that displays unwanted advertisements on a computer, typically as pop-up windows. While adware can be annoying, it is not typically considered a security threat.

Question 12:

Answer: C.

Ext4 is a journaling file system for Linux that supports large file systems, extended attributes, and efficient data storage. Journaling is a feature that keeps track of changes to the file system and can help recover data in case of a crash or power failure. Journaling file systems are more reliable than non-journaling file systems, and the Ext4 file system is one of the most commonly used journaling file systems for Linux.

- FAT32: FAT32 is a file system used by Microsoft Windows and other operating systems. It is not commonly used in Linux and does not support journaling.

- NTFS: NTFS is the file system used by Microsoft Windows. It is not commonly used in Linux and does not support journaling.

- Ext4: Ext4 is a journaling file system for Linux that supports large file systems, extended attributes, and efficient data storage.

- XFS: XFS is a high-performance, journaling file system for Linux that is used for high-end storage systems. It is less commonly used than the Ext4 file system but is well suited for high-performance storage needs.

Question 13:

Answer: B.

A drive-by download is a type of malware that infects a computer when a user visits a malicious website or clicks on a malicious link. The user does not have to take any action other than visiting the website, and the malware is downloaded and installed automatically. Public kiosks, such as those found in hotels, airports, and other public places, are often prime targets for drive-by downloads.

• Social Engineering: Social engineering is a type of attack that uses trickery and deceit to gain access to sensitive information or systems. It does not involve automatically downloading malware through visiting a website.

• Rogue software: Rogue software is a type of malicious software that is disguised as legitimate software and is often used to steal sensitive information or take control of a system.

• Drive-by downloads: A drive-by download is a type of malware that infects a computer when a user visits a malicious website or clicks on a malicious link.

• Phishing Scams: Phishing scams are attacks that attempt to trick the user into providing sensitive information, such as passwords or credit card numbers, by disguising themselves as a trusted source, such as a bank or other financial institution.

Question 14:

Answer: D.

The best category for this type of file is Archived data.

Archived data refers to information that is no longer actively used but is still needed for historical or regulatory purposes. The addition of metadata to product documentation files for long-term data classification and archiving purposes fits this definition, as the information will be stored for future reference but may not be actively used.

Confidential files refer to information that is sensitive and should only be accessible by authorized individuals. Marketing collateral refers to promotional materials used to support the marketing of a product. Engineering specifications refer to detailed technical information used in the design and development of a product. Neither of these categories accurately describes the type of file being added metadata to for archiving purposes.

Question 15:

Answer: B.

A Solid State Drive (SSD) is a type of storage device that uses flash memory to store data. Unlike a Hard Disk Drive (HDD), which uses rotating disks to read and write data, SSDs have no moving parts and access data much more quickly. This makes SSDs generally faster than HDDs when it comes to disk read and write operations. Hybrid drives (HDD/SSD) offer a combination of both traditional hard disk storage and flash-based storage, while Optical Disk Drives (ODDs) are used to read CDs, DVDs, and Blu-Ray disks, but are not typically used for storage.

Question 16:

Cindy needs to describe ransomware to her boss. What explanation should she use?

5.   Ransomware is a type of malicious software that infects a computer system and restricts access to its files and data, typically by encrypting them. The attacker then demands payment in exchange for a decryption key to restore access to the affected data.

6.   Ransomware is a type of spyware that tracks the user's online activity and reports it back to the attacker.

7.   Ransomware is a type of malware that deletes the user's files and data permanently.

8.   Ransomware is a type of adware that displays unwanted advertisements and pop-ups on the user's computer.

Answer: A.

Ransomware is a type of malicious software that infects a computer system and restricts access to its files and data, typically by encrypting them. The attacker then demands payment in exchange for a decryption key to restore access to the affected data. This explanation accurately describes the behavior of ransomware and the consequences for the user.

Question 17:

Answer: C.

The term that best describes cloud software that does not need to be installed but instead runs within a web browser is SaaS (Software as a Service).

SaaS refers to a delivery model for software where the software is hosted in the cloud and made available to customers over the internet. The customers do not need to install the software on their own computers, but instead access it through a web browser. This means that the software is always up-to-date and can be accessed from anywhere with an internet connection.

SECaaS (Security as a Service) refers to a cloud-based service that provides security solutions, such as firewalls, antivirus software, and intrusion detection systems.

IaaS (Infrastructure as a Service) refers to a cloud-based delivery model for infrastructure services, such as storage, computing power, and networking.

PaaS (Platform as a Service) refers to a cloud-based delivery model for platform services, such as databases, application servers, and development tools.

Question 18:

Answer: B.

The most likely problem is that the website has been infected with malware.

A website that displays pop-up ads and is slow to load may be infected with malware, which can harm visitors' workstations by transmitting viruses or other malicious software. Pop-up ads are often used to spread malware, and a slow-loading web site may indicate that the site's servers are bogged down with excessive traffic or are trying to execute malicious code.

In contrast, a corrupted workstation DNS cache would not cause pop-up ads or slow site performance. A DNS cache is used to store the IP addresses of frequently visited web sites for faster access, and if it is corrupted, it can cause issues with website resolution. However, this would not result in pop-up ads or slow site performance.

An expired web site certificate could result in a warning or error message when accessing the site, but it would not cause pop-up ads or slow site performance. Web site certificates are used to encrypt data transmitted between the site and the visitor's browser, and an expired certificate indicates that the site is no longer secure.

Question 19:

Answer: E.

Fully Encrypting the hard drive makes the data stored on it unreadable to unauthorized users. If the laptop is lost or stolen, the encrypted data will not be accessible without the correct encryption key. Installing anti-virus software is important to prevent malware infections, but it will not protect against data theft if the laptop is lost or stolen. Requiring a password to access the laptop provides basic security, but it does not prevent unauthorized access to the data stored on the laptop. Keeping sensitive information on a separate device is a good security practice, but it does not protect the data on the lost laptop.

Question 20:

Answer: B.

Laser printers are known for their high-quality printing, high speed, and versatility. They can handle a wide variety of paper types and are very reliable. The high-quality printing and versatility of laser printers make them a popular choice in offices. Because they use toner rather than ink, they are also very efficient and can produce high volumes of prints. In this case, the user was able to resolve the printing issue by switching to a different type of paper, which suggests that the printer is a laser printer.

Question 21:

Answer: B.

A column-oriented database management system is optimized for processing and storing large amounts of structured data that can be organized into columns. This type of database management system is well suited for web applications like news sites, where vast amounts of data such as user comments, links, and embedded files need to be processed and stored in a way that can be easily queried and analyzed. Unlike traditional relational database management systems, column-oriented databases store data in columns rather than rows, making them more efficient for large-scale data storage and retrieval operations.

Question 22:

Answer: A, D.

The correct options are:

- Break the data down into smaller fields

- Break the data down into smaller columns

The customer data stored in the relational database should be broken down into smaller fields and columns to ensure faster search performance. Splitting the "Customer Name" field into separate fields for first name and last name allows for quicker and more efficient searches as the database can now be searched based on either first or last name without having to search the entire "Customer Name" field.

Breaking the data down into smaller fields also makes it easier to manipulate and manage the data as it can be sorted and filtered based on specific field values.

Additionally, this will also help in avoiding data duplication and maintaining the integrity of the customer data stored in the database.

Breaking the data down into smaller rows or records is not necessary and would actually slow down the search performance as it would increase the number of rows or records in the database, making the search process more complex and time-consuming.

Question 23:

Answer: C.

The correct data type for this variable would be a string (String).

The reason for this is that mobile phone numbers are a combination of numerical and non-numeric characters (e.g. +, -, (,), and spaces), and therefore cannot be stored as an integer or float data type. A string data type can store characters, and is a better choice for storing mobile phone numbers because it can handle the non-numeric characters and spaces in phone numbers.

Boolean is a data type that can only store true or false values and is not appropriate for storing mobile phone numbers.

Question 24:

Answer: B.

For the Items In Stock column in a relational database design for a retail chain that sells prank items, the appropriate data type to choose would be Integer. This is because the column will be storing a numerical value that represents the quantity of a particular item that is in stock. A Boolean data type is used for binary values (true or false), a Float data type is used for decimal values, and a String data type is used for character data. However, in this case, a numerical value is needed to accurately represent the quantity of an item in stock, making the Integer data type the most suitable choice.

Question 25:

Answer: A.

In order to send a fax using a Plain Old Telephone Service (POTS), a fax machine requires a modem. The modem converts the digital signals generated by the fax machine into analog signals that can be transmitted over the POTS network. Without a modem, the fax machine would not be able to communicate over the telephone network and therefore could not send a fax.

Question 26:

Answer: C.

Change the administrator password

The first management configuration that Aria should do is to change the administrator password. This is important for security reasons as the default password for the router is usually easily accessible and can be found online. By changing the password, Aria ensures that only she or authorized users have access to the router's settings and configuration. This will prevent unauthorized access to the network, unauthorized changes to the network settings, and protect against malicious attacks.

Question 27:

Answer: D.

The software development life cycle (SDLC) is a process for creating and maintaining software. During the maintenance phase, software security fixes are created and made available to consumers. This is because security vulnerabilities may be discovered after the software has been released and is in use. The maintenance phase is important for ensuring the long-term security and stability of the software.

Question 28:

Answer: C.

Before John can locate Wi-Fi networks and connect to one, he must turn on Wi-Fi on the device. The Wi-Fi switch is usually found in the Settings app or the Control Center, depending on the device and its operating system version. Turning on Wi-Fi will allow the device to scan for available Wi-Fi networks and show a list of available Wi-Fi networks that can be connected to.

Question 29:

Answer: B, D.

Disable Bluetooth and Wi-Fi.

Bluetooth and Wi-Fi both have the potential to be exploited by attackers as they are wireless protocols. Disabling them will minimize the attack surface and reduce the risk of unauthorized access to the device. Additionally, it is advisable to keep Location Services and GPS turned off when not in use, as they can reveal sensitive information such as the device's location. Mobile data can still be used to connect to the internet if necessary, but it is best to use it only when required and keep security measures such as encryption enabled.

Question 30:

Answer: B.

Requirements gathering and analysis is the first step in the software development life cycle (SDLC) where stakeholders, customers and end-users are consulted to identify the needs and requirements of the software solution. This phase helps in defining the scope of the project and provides a roadmap for the subsequent phases of design, implementation, testing, deployment, and maintenance.

Conclusion

In the journey through the CompTIA IT Fundamentals (ITF+) Practice Questions, we've explored a comprehensive array of topics crucial for building a foundational understanding of information technology. From the intricacies of IT concepts and terminology to delving into infrastructure, applications and software, software development, database fundamentals, and security, this book has been designed to be a valuable resource for IT enthusiasts, students, and professionals preparing for the ITF+ exam.

Navigating the Chapters:

Chapter 1 - IT Concepts and Terminology: We began by establishing a solid understanding of notational systems, data representation, fundamental data types, and the basics of computing and processing.

Chapter 2 - Infrastructure: We then delved into the classification of input/output device interfaces, the installation of common peripheral devices, and the purpose of internal computing components.

Chapter 3 - Applications and Software: This chapter elucidated the role of operating systems, components of an operating system, the purpose of software, application architecture, and the configuration of web browsers.

Chapter 4 - Software Development Concepts: Here, we compared programming language categories, delved into programming organizational techniques, and explored programming concepts.

Chapter 5 - Database Fundamentals: This chapter explored database concepts, structures, and methods used to interface with databases.

Chapter 6 - Security: Finally, we comprehensively covered security concepts, encryption, business continuity, and common password best practices.

Practice Questions:

To solidify your understanding, we provided 30 practice questions per chapter with detailed explanations for each answer. These questions are designed to simulate the exam environment and test your grasp of the material.

Moving Forward:

As you embark on your IT journey, whether it be for academic pursuits, certification exams, or professional development, remember that continuous learning is key.

Technology evolves rapidly, and staying current with industry trends and advancements will set you on a path to success.

We hope this book has been a valuable companion in your ITF+ exam preparation, offering clarity on essential concepts and providing a platform for self-assessment. Good luck on your journey, and may your passion for information technology continue to grow and thrive!